How to give your users the LIS services they want

Sheila Pantry OBE and Peter Griffiths

facet publishing

© Sheila Pantry and Peter Griffiths 2009

Published by Facet Publishing
7 Ridgmount Street, London WC1E 7AE
www.facetpublishing.co.uk

Facet Publishing is wholly owned by CILIP: the Chartered Institute of Library and
Information Professionals.

Sheila Pantry and Peter Griffiths have asserted their right under the Copyright, Designs and
Patents Act 1988 to be identified as authors of this work.

British Library Cataloguing in Publication Data
A catalogue record for this book is available from the British Library.

ISBN 978-1-85604-672-5

First published 2009

Text printed on FSC accredited material.

Mixed Sources
Product group from well-managed
forests and other controlled sources
www.fsc.org Cert no. SA-COC-1565
© 1996 Forest Stewardship Council

Typeset from author's files in 11/15pt Classical Garamond and Franklin Gothic by
Facet Publishing.

Printed and made in Great Britain by MPG Books Group, UK.

How to give your users the LIS services they want

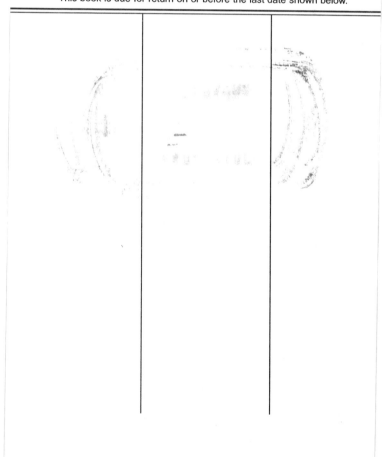

By the same authors:

By Sheila Pantry OBE and Peter Griffiths

Becoming a Successful Intrapreneur: a practical guide to creating an innovative information service
ISBN 978-1-85604-292-5

Developing a Successful Service Plan
ISBN 978-1-85604-392-2

Managing Outsourcing in Library and Information Services
ISBN 978-1-85604-543-8

Setting up a Library and Information Service from Scratch
ISBN 978-1-85604-558-2

Your Essential Guide to Career Success 2nd edn
ISBN 978-1-85604-491-2

By Sheila Pantry OBE

Managing Stress and Conflict in Libraries
ISBN 978-1-85604-613-8

By Peter Griffiths

Managing your Internet and Intranet Services, 2nd edn
ISBN 978-1-85604-483-7

Contents

Preface

THIS BOOK AIMS to help library and information services (LIS) workers at all levels and in all industry sectors in the UK and globally to survive and thrive in the 21st century. 'All levels' include those in careers spread across all sectors of library and information work (such as local government, private or 'special' and academic libraries) and electronic information related posts such as webmasters and knowledge managers. We intend that – like our other titles – this book will be useful to an international audience.

We believe that there is still a lot of potential to reach users through changing methods of communication, and electronic information workers and digital librarians have some more work to do. You can track people through websites, but it is more difficult to understand *why* they navigate the way they do as well as seeing *where* they navigate.

Keep in touch with any new user or user group and track their behaviour to see if new patterns of behaviour are forming. Watch what other industries such as publishing are doing to make their users come to them. Expand your activities to cover online networks, digital libraries and other forms of social networking.

We encourage all information workers to constantly think 'out of the LIS box' – looking at your LIS with new eyes and new knowledge at all times, and find out how to stay ahead of the game.

Sheila Pantry
Peter Griffiths

1

Why this book?

In these turbulent times, library and information service (LIS) staff at all levels need constantly to keep one step, or more, ahead of the users.

Today's LIS users do not behave like those who used the services ten or twenty years ago, and today's user behaviour will change again, probably even more rapidly than we have seen in recent years. Having the strategies to deal with this is not just an issue for senior managers and the leaders of the profession. Nor is it just an issue for the public library sector. It is an issue for every type of library, and for library and information professionals at every level – and in every country.

While we recognize that nothing stands still in this information world of ours, we believe that the focus of all our attention remains (and always has been) the user. Without users there is no real reason for a library and information service to exist. Experience will give the manager an advantage – but do we need to get older to be able to assess and forecast what the users will do next as far as information searching, retrieval and subsequent usage of the data is concerned? LISs worldwide spend enormous sums of money on staff, purchasing services, materials and other systems, but do they really understand what exactly makes the user tick?

In recent years many ideas, often from other sectors, have taken off and been exploited in new and exciting ways. They are being communicated in real time to world wide audiences. Many new applications are being developed quickly on the back of this for services such as Facebook, MySpace, Twitter and Google Maps. Major trends are emerging and converging, such as Twittering and mash-ups, conversations and open linked data. And at last the semantic web is becoming a reality as more organizations publish their data in open formats that these new tools can access and exploit creatively across the web. Everyone in the marketplace can participate, including publishers, library and information centres and users. Many people who never entered an LIS are participating and the information world of ours must shift its dynamics to embrace these new types of users. The barriers to entry are minimal – the costs of participating zero.

LISs must look for exemplar cases from around the world and renovate their services to meet the demands of 'new world information users'. You may already be involved in creating new applications for Twitter, Facebook, MySpace, Yahoo! or Google, and you may have made the move to the semantic web to deal with the digital explosion and the need to derive greater 'intelligence' from information. You may have found new ways of giving your users the LIS they want, not what you perceived them to need. And have you used new ways to transform the way your organization does its business? Do you have difficulties in changing your management processes to cope with this 'always connected' world?

Whether you work in an LIS in business, government, academia, the law or the public sector you must now be on constant alert to see if good ideas being used elsewhere can be readily transferred to your own LIS.

Defining your users

First, you will need to *agree* who are the users, so as to be able to cater adequately for their information needs now and in the future. A number of factors may influence the definition of a user of any LIS. This could be affected by agreements between your organization and others, for example agreements between local authorities, colleges or universities or businesses on a bilateral basis or as a consortium. For example in the South Yorkshire area of the UK registered open access ticket holders who live and work in the area can access all the libraries, information centres and learning centres of the local universities, colleges and public libraries. It becomes more difficult to define users, and particularly the rights they acquire through being users, when the definition lies around an organization such as a company or a college rather than a geographic area. As we shall see, licensing rules *may* make it impossible to provide full services to distance learners because of the rules imposed by the rights owners. So, not only may we find some potential users excluded, but there may be different classes of user within the same organization.

Here, for example, are some of the possible groupings of users for some of the major LIS sectors. Each will have particular requirements for potential components of an electronic information service, and the conditions of use of the service must cater for those groups.

Users in the academic sector include:

- university faculty staff
- students – on campus (undergraduate, postgraduate, doctoral)
- students – off campus (e.g. accessing university network by dial-up from local area)
- distance learning students
- disadvantaged staff and students
- research workers located elsewhere
- consultants
- information seekers who are not affiliated to the university.

Users of public libraries include:

- members of the public, including students and children
- people who work in the area
- businesses
- researchers

- users of specified collections
- distance learning students.

Users of private sector information services include:

- own staff, in principal business premises
- own staff, in other business premises (e.g. overseas offices)
- own staff, on business travel (e.g. dial-up from clients' premises or hotel)
- users from other information centres and libraries belonging to a local co-operative with whom there is a reciprocal agreement; use may be granted – perhaps in a limited way
- secondees working for the company or organization (employees of other organizations on the company's premises).

Users of government information services include:

- own department or agency staff
- researchers working for the department or agency
- other government departments' or agencies' staff
- consultants
- the general public.

Some of these groups will contain users who wish to find information in order to republish it, e.g. in research documents or as journalism. This will also have an impact on the level of service that can be offered.

We must not forget the results of recent research into the information seeking behaviour of students that can be found in the CIBER briefing paper *Information Behaviour of the Researcher of the Future* (CIBER, 2008). CIBER conducted this research for the British Library and Joint Information Systems Committee (JISC). The report focuses on information seeking behaviour of students born after 1993 (the Google Generation). The paper also ties in research from OCLC's study on students' perceptions (OCLC, 2006).

So what are the main challenges to libraries and their information services in meeting the needs of tomorrow's scholars and researchers?

We think it worth dealing fully with the challenges for us all that were identified as the conclusions of the CIBER report (33–4):

1. Taking full advantage of the popularity of scholarly information and at the same time dealing with the fact that UK users are the **minority group** for many UK-funded, cash-strapped information services.

2. Reversing the process of **dis-intermediation** in a full-blown do-it-yourself consumer marketplace. As they say 'we are all librarians now'. For instance, how to sell the key library role of a safe and authoritative information haven and the need for digital information literacy training. Libraries are handicapped here by a lack of brand, although there is evidence that the BL has a good international presence. Publishers are better able to offer something here with their strong commercial and academic brands and their rapidly expanding 'walled garden' information products, and strategic partnerships should be considered.

3. Becoming much more **e-consumer-friendly** and less stodgy and intellectual. Few digital library offerings make any real attempt to connect with the larger digital consumer world: they simply do not chime with people's experience of Facebook, YouTube, Amazon or even for that matter, ScienceDirect. Why, for example, don't academic libraries try to emulate personal/social searching guidance offered so successfully by Amazon for many years?

4. Avoiding the **decoupling scenario** – libraries being decoupled from the user and the publisher. With the arrival of the e-book libraries will become even more remote from their users and publishers will become even closer as a result of consumer footfalls occurring in their domain. The fall out with publishers over open access and institutional repositories has caused a schism between librarians and publishers and the increasing willingness of the user to pay for information (a trend noticed by all publishers) will increase the isolation of libraries.

5. Introducing robust, fit-for-purpose mechanisms for monitoring and **evaluating their users** (and information services). Faced with the prospect that the future scholar will only ever want to use them remotely it is absolutely crucial that libraries have a means of monitoring and evaluating what they do. Furthermore, it is not sufficient to just listen and monitor it is also necessary to change in response to this data. Otherwise libraries will be increasingly marginalized and anonomized in the virtual information world. No private sector corporation would survive on the basis of failing to invest in consumer profiling, market research and loyalty programmes. No library we are aware of has a department devoted to the evaluation of the user, how can that be?

6. Really getting **information skills** on the agenda because clearly people are having great difficulties navigating and profiting from the virtual scholarly environment. To succeed it will be necessary to lead on outcomes/benefits (better researchers, degrees etc) and work closely with publishers.

7. The library profession desperately needs leadership to develop a new vision for the 21st century and reverse its declining profile and influence. This should start with effecting that shift from a content-orientation to a user-facing perspective and then on to an **outcome focus**.

So this book looks at a wide range of topics starting with Chapter 2: 'Understanding users – the what, why, where, when, how and who'. We ask what services users need or should have; why we in the information profession need to know about our users and their behaviour; where users are and how this affects their ideas of good service; when to talk to users about their information needs; how users obtain information and how to assess these ways; who you need to consider when planning and performing the audit – managers are customers too – and finally we ask simply: What next?

In Chapter 3 we look at the current knowledge of user behaviour and needs and ask whether it is really predictable. We suggest ways of discovering your users – who are they and where they are, and we give some ideas by identifying some potential categories of user, e.g. students, lecturers, and business, technical, scientific and medical users.

The task of the LIS manager is to achieve defined objectives. A simplistic statement, perhaps, but it is rare that such objectives are set out in any terms other than the broadest – for example, 'to meet the needs of its users'. In fact, the definition of objectives in any service organization is likely to be an iterative process that both adds precision to and takes account of emerging requirements such as those produced by emerging technologies. But however these changing requirements are handled, the explicit responsibility to meet users' needs requires the manager and his or her staff to examine user behaviour as a first step to determining policy.

In Chapter 4 we discuss the levels of users and their expectations and where the role of the information professional and user training interacts. Throughout the book we are trying to encourage LIS managers and staff to 'think outside the LIS box' and look at your LIS with new eyes and new knowledge. Have you any new users or user groups that you could work with to track their information seeking behaviour? This is expanded to cover websites and digital libraries.

Chapter 5 asks: What information do you already hold about your users and what can you learn from their past behaviour? Past behaviour is no guarantee of future behaviour, of course, so is it worth keeping old data? There may be changes in the size or composition of your user group, and older reviews are unlikely to cover some of the services your LIS now offers, just as they may include some services that have since closed. Historic data will of course allow you to paint a picture over time of how the LIS is used, and how users regard it and its services, allowing you to track trends and comparative figures to support business cases and help with fund allocation. But there is also great value in reading the detail, because of what it tells you about the way that users have interpreted the questions put to them. You may be able not only to identify areas where jargon or lack of understanding is confusing your users (and maybe dissuading them from asking the LIS to provide a new service you would like to offer) but also gain understanding about the way that your users work and how they involve the LIS in that work.

An important by-product of reviewing what you already know will be to highlight other information stores in your organization, and this may lead you to consider whether these should be brought within your library and information service, or whether you should influence their management in any other appropriate ways.

If user surveys have been carried out before then what kind of questions did you ask in them? And most importantly what was the response? Did you make any alterations or adjust any of the services or even create a new one? This chapter gives examples of such results and offers suggestions as to what can be done to recognize future user information behaviour habits.

As always we must learn, learn and continue to learn about our users, so Chapter 6 looks at a number of opportunities: better strategic planning through analysis of user behaviour; better marketing. We discuss keeping the customers satisfied, keeping upstream management satisfied and why you should make sure that your organization recognizes the importance of its library and information service. Communications are important, too, and so is achieving cost benefits and making better use of budgets (especially in the eyes of your financial managers). We believe that all these strategic planning tasks can be better achieved using analysis of LIS user behaviour.

Library and information services do not operate in 'steady state'. They are – or should be – central to every organization irrespective of the field of activity (or 'sector' – such as academic, governmental, workplace, public, legal, financial, technical, scientific or medical LIS. In order to remain in that central role they need constantly to be assessed, evaluated and monitored, preferably by the LIS staff itself.

It will be part of your strategic planning processes for the LIS to track and evaluate the new and competing services and products that arrive on the scene. You should recognize that this is also part of your organization's strategic planning process, so user requirements should be kept in mind as part of your monitoring, planning and evaluation processes. How can this be done?

Marketing is one way that we discuss but it is also important to make the leaders of your user community aware of the assumptions or decisions you have made, and to share the information with them. This can be done succinctly: you have no need to go into every detail. In this way you can be sure that these decision makers have a summary of your evidence in front of them, and could ask for further information about particular issues of concern.

'Keeping track of changes in what users want' is discussed in Chapter 7. Here, important steps are helping users to review their information needs, learning how to keep track of changes in what users want, and identifying how and where to find information about changes in the services provided by your suppliers. The use of surveys and statistics is covered as are wider uses of information professional skills, and we look at how reputation management fits into all this.

We cannot stress too much the degree to which you should know your users and build user loyalty and strive to keep it. Finally in this chapter we ask the question 'What next?' and offer solutions!

'Each URL is a latent community – the trigger for rich and engaging conversations – the launch point for new creativity,' said Clay Shirky in his Online 2008 Keynote address (Shirky, 2008).

In Chapter 8 we look at tracking the future. We discuss how you can keep a watch on the wider changing world and what your networks can tell you. Are you using other professionals, management and technical colleagues' skills and experience enough? What are the lessons to be learnt? High on your agenda should be not only your customers' continually changing requirements but also maintaining contacts beyond your community – for example with your suppliers to be aware of developments in their worlds and the products they offer. Making use of new ways of working and partnerships is essential if the LIS is to survive.

Our final chapter, 'Future perfect?', looks forward to new levels of achievement for your LIS. We particularly recommend that readers note the advice given in *Digital Consumers* (Nicholas and Rowlands

2008). They say a new mindset is required and offer the following recommendations for the future:

1 Live with the prospect of constant change
2 Establish a link with information provision and access/outcomes
3 Keep it simple
4 Do not be seduced by digital fashions, they will all disappear.
5 Get social
6 Hold on to the physical space.

So in our final chapter we take these ideas forward and look at what could make a real difference in the future of the LIS. We give some recommendations, and ask you to consider the levels of patronage or sponsorship and what financial support you enjoy. We consider the very current issue of library as place in the context of user satisfaction, and we comment on the proposal 'Shh, this is a digital library'.

Very importantly we cover the training and development of the LIS staff and as always we cannot stress enough that all staff must have access to continuing professional development in order to meet the constant succession of changes and challenges that present themselves. When all these issues are taken into account the LIS will be able to deliver user satisfaction.

Throughout the book we have identified many actions that will contribute to giving your users the LIS they want. There are frequent challenges and opportunities to rethink your service – this time stepping 'out of the box', but part of that initiative is getting the users to articulate what they need, engaging in open dialogue with them and setting the pace by designing services from their point of view. You have access to all the information you need to keep ahead of the game if you want!

Whatever sector you work in, your LIS should be central to your community. Otherwise as is all too often seen there are dire consequences, with services cut or even decimated because the financial decision makers could not see that core value to the users.

Our conclusions are many, all based on working in various sectors

during our professional lives, observing other successful organizations – but above all our desire is to see LISs (of all kinds, and in the
widest meanings of the term) continuing to thrive and grow as they
make the most of the continuing challenges in our information
world. Enjoy!

2

Understanding users – the what, why, where, when, how and who

In this chapter we look at:

➡ the services users need or should have?
➡ why we need to know about our users and their behaviour
➡ where users are and how this affects their ideas of good service
➡ when to talk to users about their information needs
➡ how users obtain information and how to assess these ways
➡ who you need to consider when planning and performing the audit – managers are customers too.
➡ and finally – what next?

In order to get a deeper understanding of user behaviour in your LIS, we suggest that you answer a series of questions designed to examine the way that your users access and make use of information resources.

What services do LIS users need, and what should they have?

The users of an LIS as well as its managers and staff have a role to play in delivering a service, but often they are unaware of this and the service does not tell them about this role. This is what users should do to ensure that they get the best from their LIS:

• be aware of what the library and information service offers

- identify their information needs
- agree to take those needs to the LIS as first port of call
- communicate them to the information service staff and discuss them as required
- give feedback to the information service
- keep information service staff aware of their changing subject interests
- involve the information service in projects that have information implications.

This may seem easiest in an organization that has its own library, such as a university or a business, but it should be possible with a little thought to apply these criteria to all types of service. At the end of the day it is the user who really decides the quality of the services, by:

- making demands for improvements on an existing service
- asking for new services
- showing a willingness to co-operate.

However, it is not very reasonable to expect users to do this by themselves, so they may need help to describe what they need, and to contribute more generally to developing information services to suit their requirements.

You can find out what the users of your service need by carrying out an information audit to an appropriate depth and level of complexity.

The basic function of information audits is to assess a user's, community's or organization's information needs, to identify what it already holds, and to report on the gap between the two as a basis for action. The information audit is equally suited to public service and academic environments as to the workplace library services where it was first developed. It is an important and valuable technique because it yields data about the information resources held within an organization or community; it tells you how well these are matched to the information requirements of the user group; and it highlights the opportunities for intrapreneurial behaviour.

To obtain the data, the LIS manager should survey managers or other representatives (depending on the type of community being served) to gather details of the types of information that members of that community need.

This can be done by questionnaires and structured interviews; less controlled methods can be used such as sending feedback cards with library transactions but the results will probably be less reliable. The exercise should provide a clear understanding of the ways that users currently access information, and of the types of information that they use.

As well as revealing what kind of information is needed, who needs it, and the range of topics that must be covered, an information audit will also show requirements for any kind of information that is not currently available in the organization. It will help to identify any regular specialist information needs together with systems and services being used to meet those requirements. You will often find that people are using external sources such as their professional society or even the local public library because it does not occur to them to ask their own information specialists.

Information audits frequently uncover examples of poor information use that highlight the need for an information service or for improvements in existing services. The following are often found and frequently described;

- People treat information as power – but may fail to tell anyone else what information they hold.
- People keep information in databases that run on old software, which makes the databases difficult to maintain and the information difficult to share.
- People keep old information and use it as if it were current – which is dangerous.
- People get information from sources outside the organization or outside the community but don't check whether it is valid – especially if they have paid for it.
- People re-use information because they paid for it originally but it will cost them more to check that the information is still valid

– and times are tough, so they risk making a costly mistake to avoid a small outlay in order to be certain.

• People use incompatible systems, e.g. the e-mail systems that drop attachments when sending to another network, or that will not allow attachments to incoming messages through the firewall.

• People think they know how to use information resources, but actually they don't, and that leads to poor use of expensive resources.

• People duplicate work, duplicate purchases of information, and duplicate the invention of the wheel because they don't share and they don't ask before they buy.

We believe that these problems can be identified and eliminated using the information audit techniques that we cover in more detail in a number of our books. You will find sections on information audit in different contexts in *Creating a Successful E-Information Service* (Pantry and Griffiths, 2002), *Developing a Successful Service Plan* (Pantry and Griffiths, 2000), *Becoming a Successful Intrapreneur* (Pantry and Griffiths, 1998) and *Managing Outsourcing in Library and Information Services* (Pantry and Griffiths, 2004). Some of these Facet Publishing titles are out of print but they can be located in many libraries.

Defining information resources and services

In our book *The Complete Guide to Preparing and Implementing Service Level Agreements* (Pantry and Griffiths, 2nd edn, 2001) we discussed the problem of agreeing what was on offer and what users wanted. We proposed the use of a glossary or other agreed list of definitions so that there would be no ambiguity in the questions asked in the audit and in the subsequent interpretation.

We have frequently found that managers do not understand how complicated the issues are that information professionals have to deal with in purchasing and managing information, and they do not understand the terminology we use to describe those activities. Many terms have multiple definitions and multiple meanings that need to be defined. For example: do we speak of routing or circulation for journals; or does circulation involve journals (or periodicals . . .) or books (or monographs . . .); and when I say 'urgent' is that what you call 'rush'; and so on. Now bear in mind that many of the staff who let or monitor contracts do not properly understand what any of the terms mean, whichever alternative is right, and you will see the potential for chaos.

Often library and information professionals report to managers in other specialisms who may not understand the whole picture; sometimes they report to people who know nothing about our work and therefore do not understand the consequences of what we seek to do. Imagine the situation reversed: would you sanction a major re-organization of a financial or legal service if you had no idea what the service was providing because the description was ambiguous or meaningless, or couched in financial jargon you did not understand? Would your answer be the same if it was a service you did not personally use?

Having a set of definitions will help to overcome these problems, first because if everyone signs up to them then the role and operation of the LIS has been established as a common yardstick, and second because it will no longer be possible for non-LIS personnel to claim ignorance or lack of understanding. If they do not understand after signing up to a standard set of definitions, then it is their problem and the community can challenge them for failing to seek clarification.

Why we need to know about our users and their behaviour

It's important that information managers should develop a clear understanding of the entire organization or community in which the service will operate. An LIS that is driven by a vision shared only by its own staff will never be seen as important by the community or organization that it serves; it must be integrated into the vision of the community that supports it (because it should be an integral part of that community). The best way to achieve that is for the leaders of the LIS to be important people within their community, which in turn requires everyone in the LIS to understand how their community works and how they support it.

Before any changes are made to the service (for example in response to a discovery that customers are using it in a different way than was expected) it's important to establish the current position and record it. That way if services need to be returned to their previous state, or if it turns out that making the change has had unexpected effects on another service that need to be put right, there is a proper record of how things were. And in order to design new services or adapt existing ones, it's necessary to know what currently exists and how it's being used. (Are you putting resources into services that aren't being used; are the users going somewhere else for information; and what do they do with the information that is supplied to them?)

This is where the information audit is essential. It finds out and sets down the information needs of the users and it should also aim to identify the needs of non-users (not just because new services might attract new users but because they might help retain existing users). Your audit should not only investigate what information is being created or brought into the organization or community, but it should also seek to discover the purpose(s) to which information is being put. That may reveal more effective alternative sources of information that the service currently provides, and it may reveal new sources and information types that are wanted by users and potential users but not yet supplied.

We shall give you a short account of the methods used in information auditing a little later in this chapter, when we come to the *how* of understanding your user community. But before you can carry out an audit, you need to have a good understanding of the geography of your user community because it may well affect the kind of information they want, the ways they seek it, and the ways in which you can provide it (for example because licences restrict the locations where you can offer electronic access to journals).

Where are the users of the service? How does this affect their ideas and expectations of good service?

It will prove easier to offer good quality information services once you have a clear idea of where users and potential users are located – in terms of geography and organizational structure. Geographic location can affect your ability to network information services and will therefore affect costs; while in too many cases the politics of organizations can prove an obstacle to providing information services if you ignore hierarchies and departmental boundaries when supporting clients within a community.

A number of assumptions about users are embedded in the design of various types of library and information services. Some types of library and information service have to make assumptions about the people who are using their services, and probably have rules that restrict the user group and the subject coverage of the collection. This is pretty obvious: public libraries are primarily for the use of people who live, work or study in their area – and the people who fund the service through their local taxes would want it to be that way – libraries in education specialize in the subjects taught in their institutions, and workplace libraries are not generally available to people outside the organization that houses them. But there are more subtle factors in play.

Local authorities make a number of unstated assumptions about facilities in their branches, in particular that large branches will provide better facilities than small branches. Small branches are more likely to be situated in residential areas, however, and therefore are generally nearer to the majority of users than large central libraries in shopping centres and other non-residential areas.

Users of smaller libraries may have different or lower expectations and their requirements may be professionally more mundane (though no less valued) yet they (and sometimes Members) regard the concentration of services in larger libraries as wrong. Why should they have to travel? Why should the people in that area have it all? 'Concentrations,' following any local government reorganization are particularly sensitive. We all want a local service but this is not usually affordable.

Extract from evidence by Ealing Library and Information Service to the *DNH Public Library Review* (1995)

So there is potential tension between, on one hand, the users' desire for a service close to their homes and, on the other, the library's expectation that users wanting more than a basic fiction lending and quick reference service will either accept slower service or will travel to a central point. Recently many users have taken their expectations to Google instead.

Understandably, special libraries tend to be designed around the needs of the parent body. However, business organizations operate in pursuit of business objectives rather than public service, which in a library context may mean premises that are less than suitable. It may also mean that the business is located in separate buildings rather than in one convenient place where all your users are together. Worse, the information service may be in one building and the biggest user group in another. There may be additional budget costs for courier services and for additional licensing costs over multiple sites. The library may suffer because corporate space planning ignores it and the best location may be unavailable or remote from users. This does not take away the user requirement, and the library may find that users have higher expectations than it is able to fulfil due to physical constraints.

Academic libraries suffer less from these issues; students and staff are used to the idea of a concentration of information and resources in a single large building, or a series of independent but linked and related collections such as are found in the colleges of Oxford University. A feeling of constant evolution is engendered by innovations such as information commons and heavy investment in e-journals and IT. Is it now assumed that users receive equal service whether on or off campus? Based on their experience of web search, users are observed (Bawden and Vilar, 2006) to have unrealistic expectations of digital library collections.

Research also suggests that users expect library services to look and behave like the search engines and internet resources that they use constantly (Ponsford and van Duinkerken, 2007). Is this reasonable in your community? It may be possible to install one of the major search engines as a front end but this costs money. But knowing that this is an issue for your users makes it possible to address the point, both by considering whether any changes can be made and by highlighting the opportunity to train and inform users about the library system – including its apparent shortcomings. Users may not realize that (unlike their free use of internet search engines) library systems have to be paid for.

In Chapter 3 we shall look further at the question of where users are.

When to talk to users about their information needs

The simple answer to this question is: continually. Information service users live in a wider world where communications are constant and targeted to their interests and concerns. Their information needs are in continual evolution, and so are the methods of information delivery. Dempsey (2009) comments that users are finding the formal IT environments of their workplace or university 'increasingly clunky' compared with what they have at home; while the 'always-on' functionality of smart phones (such as the BlackBerry and iPhone) raises expectations of information being available at all times, wherever the user happens to be at the time. In an earlier article Dempsey (2006) also notes that users increasingly expect to find resources available on the web, which effectively means that they expect to find them through Google.

So it is never too late or too early to talk to users about information needs. They have to be told that the universe of knowledge is not available for free via their chosen search engine, and that there are some basic safety procedures to be followed when using information. They have to be trained to define the information they need, and to describe what they have access to through various channels.

The extensive list of questions and your discussions may well uncover poor information management habits. Your task as the manager of the library or information centre is to introduce awareness and training programmes that tackle and eliminate these habits by showing the members of your community how to use your valuable resources. You will find a growing body of helpful advice on this subject, which has become known as 'information literacy'.

There is already a considerable body of literature available to give you some idea of what users like and dislike about their library services. A combination of search engine and database searches will readily provide evidence (of varying levels of reliability) that could inspire some useful questions for your audit. The key issue is not to assume that users are going to continue to behave as they have until now.

How users obtain information and how to assess their habits

So we have established that users obtain information from a variety of sources and have varying levels of skill in interpreting what they find. As we said above, we believe that information audits are the tool that will unearth the wealth of data that will ensure that the services you design and deliver are effective in meeting your users' needs by focusing on the most relevant sources and tackling the most common and off-putting misconceptions among your community about information resources.

Over the years we have developed a range of pertinent questions that should be put to a representative selection of users and non-users. In addition you can use less reliable methods such as feedback questionnaires (less reliable because they will probably be filled in by your most consistent users rather than non-users). Here is a selection of questions that can be used; they supplement the questions in Chapter 2.

- Which information resources do you believe support the organization's aims and objectives and its programme of work?

(or the community's activities, or whatever is a relevant version of this question).

- Can you categorize these information sources into the following groups: essential; desirable; nice to have?
- Where (in which departments or with which people) does the information reside?
- Where is it obtained from (or where is it created)?
- How up to date is it, and how is it maintained (both its contents and to ensure all copies are the same)?
- What format(s) is the information available in? Can the format(s) be easily used by the organization's process and systems?
- When is it needed and is it readily available when required?
- Where are the gaps in existing information flows and currently held information?
- As well as these gaps, what other major information needs exist?
- How many sections within the organization or the community being served have their own collections of information, and which of these have an official branch of the information service?
- How many different computer based information systems are in use already?
- Are there other potential users for existing information?
- Are there potential users who cannot obtain the information they need (or believe they need) within the organization?
- Why do people use a particular service or source of information in preference to others?
- How many people in the community use externally based information services already, e.g. online databases, the internet, e-sources?
- Why do some people use the service frequently, some occasionally and some never?
- Are all community members fully trained and able to use the computerized services and technologies?
- If not, how much training is needed and at what level?
- What other training is needed for LIS staff and users?

- Finally, ask individuals the question: 'On what information do you depend to carry out your job (or any regular activity in the community)?'

Having the answers to these questions will allow the LIS manager to begin to select or design a range of services that will meet the needs of the greatest number of users in the most cost-effective way. But remember that it can take considerable time from initial consultation and information audit to achieve the final outcomes in the form of new or revised services. It was reported for example that an audit at the UK Royal College of Nursing (RCN) took a full two years to complete and implement (Hyams, 2001). See the RCN information needs survey of nurses published in 2005 (RCN, 2005).

A caveat – audit issues outside the scope of this book

Your information audit is likely to reveal a number of issues that may be quite worrying: the use of poor quality information, bad habits of data storage such as potential breaches of data protection, or unwarranted risks in storing and backing up information. This would lead you to ask some important questions that unfortunately lie outside the scope of this book. We suggest that once you have looked at the information management questions in the list above you should then consider some or all of the following more specialized questions:

Questions about ethics:

- Are we legal (do we comply with copyright law and freedom of information and data protection regulations)?

Questions about information standards:

- Is the information in the best format for future storage? If not, what has to be done?

- How long will our current standards last before they need replacement?

Questions about information management:

- How do we identify all the copies of the information and decide which one is the master? How do we stop future variants being created?
- Is there sufficient metadata and other information to describe and retrieve the information?
- How long are we going to keep this information and how will we dispose of it? (Bear in mind for example that you may destroy a master record but it will persist on back-up copies for several months or even years.)

Questions about information assurance:

- What are the risks to the information? What rules are there about access, amendment and destruction? How do we know that nobody has maliciously changed it? In short, what is our information assurance policy?

Questions about business continuity:

- How would we cope if we lost our e-journals? (Loss of data links can be catastrophic.)

The definition of information audit is constantly evolving. Early case studies in the 1990s reflect information audit as a business process and the identification of resources. This is still an important aspect but the growth of information assurance has given the subject a new dimension. Audit has now extended to assessing the integrity of information and the risk to information and its users, for example where someone has deliberately altered statistics or statements for a malicious purpose. At the same time we are seeing documents with titles such as 'Information needs analysis', which overlap with the definition of information audit. We shall continue to keep watch on this area.

Who do you need to consider when planning and performing the audit?

So, an information audit seeks to answer a number of questions about information and its use in the organization. Some of these questions should convince management (or the people funding the service) of the value of time and effort spent on the information audit activity. And as we just saw, it will highlight those areas where poor use is being made of costly resources.

But what if you need to convince management that an information audit, which can be costly in time and effort, is needed? The key questions below address the most disruptive of the poor information habits that we have been looking at. Are there positive answers to all these questions? There should be if the decision is to do without an information audit.

Some of these questions resemble the ones in the full audit, so you could use the responses as part of the main exercise. It would do no harm if your interviewee were aware of that, and could see him or herself as a pathfinder or champion by agreeing to go first. These are the most important questions to ask:

- Are you certain that there is effective control of information resources and the organization's (or the community's) expenditure on them?
- Can you say what the users' main information needs are and whether they are satisfied?
- Is the information scattered around a number of computer systems? Do you know where the accurate copy is?
- How many staff use external based information services already, e.g. online databases, the internet, e-resources? Are these better than internal sources? What external information services do you – and your users – have access to? Do you have, or need, a

budget to access or buy information? How much is all this costing?
- Are all users fully trained and able to use the computerized services and technologies?

Outcomes: benefits for the LIS

Information audits have benefits for the LIS as well as the organization or community. When the findings are analysed the LIS will:

- know how well the service and its products are perceived – or not!
- know the organization's real information needs
- find out where its users are in the organization
- understand why people in the organization go elsewhere for information
- have identified priority consumers of information, including those not currently making use of the service
- know how to provide information where and when needed, and in the required formats
- have results that will help to target future publicity.

The added bonus is that the knowledge that the information centre staff gain about the organization from doing the audit will increase their standing in the community.

Outcomes: building and keeping user loyalty

You cannot take user loyalty for granted. There are more sources every day that they can use instead of your service. If this is not to become a problem then you need to take positive action to keep your users as loyal customers of your (and their) LIS rather than of the latest search engine or social networking website. Based on experience, here are our thoughts on what will keep your users coming back to you:

- Users like to be consulted: do it before, during and after your service or product is available.
- Users like customer care in all its aspects: e-mails, telephone calls, focus groups, etc. Keep up to date with the latest networking tools and use them where appropriate to reach your leading edge users.
- Users tell others about their experiences – so give them something positive to tell them about.
- Users will let you know what the competition is doing, and how well, even if they do that while criticizing you.
- Users will tell you about new services that they want you to provide – hopefully you will already have heard about them . . .
- Users like to have contact with a staff member they know – think about the way account managers operate in public relations or personnel.
- Users do not like changes without consultation – so make sure that your communications are excellent!

Outcomes: improve your communications!

As we have just indicated, communication is an essential part of an information audit. People need to know what is going on, why it is happening and what is likely to happen afterwards. When the benefits start to be felt, people should be told what has been achieved and left in no doubt that this is down to the work done by the LIS. There need to be positive incentives for people to switch to your new ways of doing things, and one good way of doing this is to tell them about the successes that they could be part of.

What new items of information has your work created? These could be:

- descriptive documents setting out the way information is managed in the community
- statements of information requirements around the organization,

which could be shared with those just starting to define what they want
- statements saying what is available within the organization, but including any notes about restrictions because of security, licences or other factors
- an analysis of the difference between these two sets of statements – a gap analysis
- recommendations on providing further information services or on changes in information technology management that could assist information users
- the business cases used to justify access to information services.

Sharing these will help other information users (actual or potential) as well as demonstrating to the key decision makers in your user community that the information service means business. Even better, the documents should show that the information service is listening to its customers, and publishing them will prove it.

Your full information audit report is likely to be too long for many of your senior users to have the time or inclination to read it. Summarize it to bring out the salient points. Don't just make this a short report – two pages of A4 should be your limit – but create a presentation as well. Your intranet is a good channel for making this available to everyone and you can send e-mails to your key decision makers containing a link to the report. If you are working in a non-corporate environment so there is no intranet, consider putting this information onto an internet website.

Endorsement by your senior users will make your audit even more effective so make sure that they see it and tell you that they support it.

Who you need to consider – managers are customers too

What do your managers think you do in your LIS? Sometimes the service is overseen by a non-specialist committee or steering group, or it may be headed by a manager who has not been trained in the information profession. As a result the service may be governed by people who do not always appreciate what is entailed in running an information service. The belief that all information is freely available on the internet has led in recent years to closures of information centres, because in the absence of better understanding it has seemed obvious that savings were to be made. This argument clearly overlooks the risk to businesses and communities from bad information, but is attractive if a budget has to be balanced. How have managers come to have this mistaken view of information services and their value?

Information services should be central to every organization irrespective of the field of activity (or 'sector' – that is, academic, government, workplace, public, legal, financial, technical, scientific or medical). At some time in the lifetime of all information services questions should be asked about their role, function, effectiveness and cost benefit to their users; it is especially useful to do this at the outset when setting up a new service, new library or information centre, or when appraising or reviewing the current services. It is also important to do this when building electronic services for a sometimes unseen audience. But this does not mean tearing down the old service before any work has been done to establish information needs; consider risk as well as cost, and weigh the relative merits of existing and proposed services.

Managers are customers too. This means that as well as meeting the more modest demands of the organization or community at large, the LIS should aim to meet the requirements of its managers whether or not the managers have learnt how to define and express them. Elected members and senior officers can make good use of targeted information and news related to their responsibilities, although they might not recognize this. Managers are also customers for well constructed business plans, and for effective demonstrations of the way that library and information services save the community's resources.

Consider building up a store of case studies showing how the LIS has contributed to the organization's effectiveness, including its financial effectiveness. Show how having a vital fact to hand, or being able to access a particular resource, has led to a better outcome. If you are really lucky you may get someone to share their disaster with you, and show how lacking the vital fact or resource led to bad decisions and loss.

What next?

The answer to this final question is simple: get ready to do it again. Information needs and information resources both develop constantly, so what was a good match can become less good. Go to see your heaviest users at frequent intervals and others as often as you can manage. Use the questionnaires as a basis to see what has altered and what has remained the same – and adjust your services accordingly!

Summary

Keep in mind Kipling's Serving Men and ask continual questions so that you always understand your users' current needs. The information audit is a valuable tool to support you, but it needs to be carefully put together and to be repeated at intervals to ensure that the findings remain valid.

User expectations are changing at an alarming rate because of social networking and other new (Web 2.0) technologies. Users behave very differently from their ways of only five years ago, although other aspects of user behaviour remain consistent, such as going to colleagues before they consult the library. Read widely, stay in touch with technological developments, and talk to your users in order to see where new or redesigned services could attract or retain them. Use effective messages to tell users when their expectations are unreasonable (for legal or financial reasons) and to show them that the LIS can offer more reliable and better targeted information than they can get from internet search engines.

Communication is an essential tool in helping to take news about the service, as well as the arguments in favour of giving it proper resources, to the opinion makers. Remember that managers are potential or actual users of the service, and that opinion formers are found among the 'low-level' users of small branch libraries as well as among the leading figures of your community.

3

What is the current knowledge about your users and their needs – is it really predictable?

In this chapter we look at:

➡ discovering your users – who are they and where are they?
➡ identifying and allocating the different categories of user, e.g. students, lecturers, and business, technical, scientific and medical users
➡ levels of user expectations
➡ whether you can predict what your users want.

The task of the LIS manager is to achieve defined objectives. A simplistic statement, perhaps, but it is rare that such objectives are set out in any terms other than the broadest – for example, 'to meet the needs of its users'. In fact, the definition of objectives in any service organization is likely to be an iterative process that adds precision to and takes account of emerging requirements such as those produced by emerging technologies. But however these changing requirements are handled, the explicit responsibility to meet users' needs requires the manager and his or her staff to examine user behaviour as a first step to determining policy.

Who and where are your users?

The introduction of electronic services widens the scope of the customer base for any LIS. The information user is no longer obliged to visit the service to interact directly, for example by browsing the shelves (which as digital resources become the norm house a rapidly diminishing proportion of the library's total stock) or meeting the staff face to face. The customers of any LIS are likely to be anyone who has access to a computer or other electronic terminal with the right software to gain entry to the remote information system and who is not excluded by your access controls.

The traditional pattern of service has been based on separate services each with a target audience, often defined by membership of another group. Thus in a single city, a public library, university library and various special libraries may have co-existed for many years. Eligibility to use the services of each would be defined by referring to certain characteristics of the users, such as where they live or work (public library), where they are educated (school or university library) or where they work (special libraries). Although in some cases permission to use another library could be created through co-operative schemes like the UK's SINTO or HATRICS, generally eligibility and membership were clearly defined and usually exclusive.

This model has rapidly become out of date for two main reasons: because electronic information services are becoming the norm, and because of the way that libraries have coped with financial and other pressures (through joint-use libraries, trusts and not-for-profit ventures, etc.).

The arrival of electronic information services has proved to be a major catalyst. The internet allows potential users to identify materials in libraries across the world and to gain access to a large number of items online. Even where full service is not available outside a controlled group, it is common for all internet users to have access to some information such as the online public access catalogue, allowing them to use the bibliographic record in another system (e.g. to generate a loan request).

Yet frequently the services offered are based on what information professionals think is happening rather than on any hard evidence about user requirements and user habits – evidence which is in short supply. Surveys continue to reflect well known user behaviours such as using informal sources in preference to formal library and information services – an observation widely made since the Neglected Resource study for the British Library almost 30 years ago (Slater, 1981). Many users persist in the belief that the internet contains the whole of human knowledge in a convenient box (Law, 1997; Griffiths, 1998). These earlier findings are reinforced by the recent CIBER briefing paper *Information Behaviour of the Researcher of the Future* (CIBER, 2008) conducted for the British Library and JISC, suggesting that efforts by the LIS community have not had much impact on entrenched attitudes.

Even more worrying, further surveys have been published suggesting contradictory behaviour. An American study of e-service use at Harvard (Goodman, 2002) found that 'users in the sciences look for current journal articles online first', but an older French survey of surveys (Muet, 1999) found that the use of electronic journals was regarded as supplementary to the use of printed originals. However, the French study did find a distinct difference between the habits of students of natural and liberal sciences. More recently, an increasing number of users are being exposed through joint-use services to facilities designed with additional audiences in mind, and the development of the concept of Information Commons places the emphasis on access regardless of format – thus making users aware of the total spectrum of information resources, and highlighting the lower relative importance of printed materials for current research and awareness when compared with the paramount importance of print in libraries 50 years ago.

These developments in service format are the second major reason why it is unwise to rely solely on the thinking associated with single-use services delivered through 'traditional' channels. Joint-use libraries are by no means a new phenomenon (in research for earlier titles we readily found examples up to 100 years old). Recently however they have provided a means of achieving efficiencies in service delivery in response to budget and other pressures, and have enabled consequential benefits to the user communities. Multi-partnership service arrangements (such as School–College–University, or

School–College–Public) sit alongside other arrangements where libraries operate in partnership with other community facilities, and user profiles are more unusual as a result of the other reasons that users come to the location.

Case study: Topping Fold

The Topping Fold library in Bury is provided as a joint venture with the Housing Service (which provided the space in a vacant shop on the estate) and the Youth Service (which was also making use of the space) (Wilkie, 2006). From the outset the service has been designed as a community resource aimed at the needs of the community on the Topping Fold estate. The Community Centre and Library (to use the full description) was the first council presence on this estate – which has had a difficult reputation – for years, but with a combination of strong local professional leadership and funding from the Big Lottery Fund a successful service has been developed featuring activities such as reading groups including parent and toddler reading sessions (STARteam), youth groups and over-50s groups. Community activities have included security advice and communal gardening, all based at the library (MLA, 2006), and in 2009 financial advice sessions began organized by the Citizens' Advice Bureau (www.time-to-read.co.uk/Toolkits/everbodys_reading/bury.asp). As a result of these and other activities the user profile is less typical of public libraries in general, and quotations from users (MLA, 2006) show that the library is attractive to users who might have been considered unwelcome customers by a less progressive service.

The customers for some services are very broadly defined. With some exceptions the library and information profession knows rather little about the users of electronic information services, and who those users or customers are (Akeroyd, 2001; Pinfield, 2001). And although vendors are adding to their electronic journal products with facilities to analyse user activity, these analyses do not (and as yet cannot) address the question of what users are looking for and whether they find it.

Customers can be the members of an organization such as a university, located either on the campus or (increasingly) remote from the faculty. In this case the LIS may need to address the difficulties raised by the conflict between the needs of alumni, who may be widely scattered, and the terms of licensing agreements.

Customers can even be the citizens of an entire geographic area:

- In Michigan, USA, the Access Michigan project gives citizens access to a range of publications through library services, libraries in commercial premises, and other public places with suitable technology. The initiative addresses specific information requirements such as health information (Brenneise and Marks, 2001), as well as providing a public electronic library (mel.org) for citizens of Michigan.
- In Iceland, an agreement reached in November 2001 gave all Icelandic citizens access to a range of journals wherever in the country they accessed the web. Under this agreement, private citizens are able to view these journals from their personal computers, in addition to the access provided from library and other institutional computers through the national portal at http://hvar.is. (Thorny Hlynsdottir and Thora Gylfadottir, 2004; Thora Gylfadottir and Thorny Hlynsdottir, 2006; van de Stadt, 2007).

To a considerable extent, therefore, the customers for services, especially electronic services, can be anyone within the LIS' target audience, and can be located anywhere that communications can be established with the LIS network. But more than this, with many library catalogues available on the internet, the audience can literally be anywhere in the world, and an important question is: does the information service want to offer any kind of service to these people beyond the ability to eavesdrop on the services offered to the intended target audience?

The 2008 CIBER briefing paper *Information Behaviour of the Researcher of the Future* casts further light on this issue in its report of research conducted for the British Library and JISC. In particular it focuses on information seeking behaviour of students born after

1993 (the Google Generation), but as widely reflected in the present book, their search behaviour is often quite different from that of previous generations and their approach to information and knowledge seeking is indicative of future requirements of library and information services. The CIBER paper reflects research from OCLC's Perceptions studies. It states:

> The research literature is inadequate in this area and what serious material there is, is eclipsed by anecdotal or unevidenced claims. The library community needs to invest more in data collection and analysis and to take its examples from commercial leaders (for example, Tesco) that have a much more detailed and insightful understanding of their customer base and preferences. In particular, there is a need for ongoing longitudinal data and intelligence functions to provide a vital early radar warning of oncoming change. Why don't major national libraries have in-house user studies departments? Without this intelligence, service stereotypes can easily become detached from reality.
>
> At national level, there is a desperate need for a well-funded programme of educational research and inquiry into the information and digital literacy skills of our young people. If the erratic behaviour we are seeing in digital libraries really is the result of failure at the library terminal, then society has a major problem. Information skills are needed more than ever and at a higher level if people are to really avail themselves of the benefits of an information society. Emerging research findings from the US points to the fact that these skills need to be inculcated during the formative years of childhood: by university or college it is too late to reverse engineer deeply ingrained habits, notably an uncritical trust in branded search engines to deliver quick fixes. This will require concerted action between libraries, schools and parents.
>
> (CIBER, 2008, 32)

These issues raise two immediate questions for the LIS professional to consider, and to ask of suppliers where appropriate:

- Access – how does the system know that it is being used by an authorized user, and how does it control the use made of the information provided?

- Intermediation – how does the librarian ensure that services meet the requirements of users when they do not need to visit the information centre?

Later we shall look at further issues where the conclusions are worrying:

- Value for money – how does the user know that he or she has found the best information, or all the information?
- Finance – how does the information service demonstrate that best value is being obtained from the system?

Categorizing your users

Do you categorize your users? Depending on your sector you may provide services to children, students, teachers or lecturers, or to business, legal, technical, scientific or medical groups. Your users, if you supply electronic services, will certainly be located somewhere else on the planet! Although your library may declare that its user group is the general public, many of these users will have particular requirements because they fall into a particular category. (Children are an obvious example here, with almost every public library providing children's literature and services, often with specialist professional staff.) So perhaps a first step would be to draw up a list of categories of user to help you identify your service's real objectives and to plan its future development. Equipped with this information your team can identify common interests among these groups that can be satisfied using the same resources, and plan services to the various user groups.

The exercise being undertaken here is known as 'segmentation' and is a widely encountered activity in marketing. A general search for information using a search engine will produce a wide range of explanatory documents based on brands in various general sales markets. An example can be found describing the market for sun creams at www.thetimes100.co.uk/downloads/nivea/nivea_11_full.pdf.

From our point of view it is interesting for including consumer categories such as 'Concerned consumers', 'Sun avoiders' and 'Naive beauty conscious', which are highly reminiscent of the names for our categories of information users as discovered during information audits.

(Great) user expectations

User expectations have grown considerably in recent years, and the traditional model of service has been largely discarded. Acceptance of a narrowly defined range of facilities at fixed hours in a single location (or a small number of places) has been superseded by an expectation of always-on ('24/7/365') delivery of innovative service coupled with an open approach to requests for new services, resources and facilities.

This has led to developments such as the information commons, combining library resources, IT resources and study space, always open for business to its user community. According to promotional material for Bailey and Tierney (2008):

> The Information Commons strives to unite all the facts and figures of the world into a resource available to everyone. Many academic libraries are considering implementing an information commons model that reflects the contemporary way patrons use resources. Others plan on revitalizing their libraries through configurations that easily integrate research, teaching, and learning with a digital focus.

Examples include the University of Sheffield (www.sheffield.ac.uk /infocommons/), Westminster College, Salt Lake City (Malenfant, 2006), and North Carolina State University (Sherman, 2008).

Meeting the library user's needs in a digital environment has been examined by Steinerova and Susol (2005) in their report *Library Users in Human Information Behaviour*, in which they aimed to study human information behaviour as part of the research project on the interaction of man and the information environment. They analysed library users' information behaviour on both sides of the information coin – information usage and information production and publishing.

The methodology was composed of the following steps: pilot studies of students' information-seeking behaviour; a large-scale questionnaire survey of users of academic and research libraries; data analyses and interpretations; verification of hypotheses; multiple data sorting; and modelling of user groups.

The findings showed that library users appreciate easy access and well organized forms of information, with an emphasis on electronic sources. In their capacity as authors of professional papers, only a few subjects considered print and electronic publishing to be equal. Two user types have been derived from the data analysis. Type S manifests pragmatic ways of information seeking and appreciates the low cost and speed of electronic publishing. Type A is characterized by analytic, in-depth information processing, stressing the prestige and review process of print publishing.

Research limitations and implications showed that quantitative methods can form a starting point for typologies of human information behaviour. Additional qualitative methods, especially interviews with students, focus groups and observations, are planned for future research into modelling of users' information behaviour. Based on the analysis, two information-seeking styles have been identified: strategic and analytic. Differences between the search styles suggest that systems designers, knowledge managers and libraries should be open to the creative use and representation of electronic information, taking into account different information behaviours.

We look at the issues that are raised by these various new approaches to library and information service in the next chapter. You will also find an extensive list of suggested further reading in addition to the references for this chapter.

Can you predict what your users want?

So how predictable are user requirements and expectations? We conclude that we are experiencing an unprecedented period of change and polarization – change as a result of rapid development in electronic information supply, new technologies such as electronic book readers (the Sony e-book, Amazon Kindle, etc.) and the ability of social networking services to act as information tools; and polarization as users fall into categories that (try as we may) it is difficult to regard other than as age-defined.

Prensky (2001) puts it thus in defining the term 'digital natives' – now otherwise known as the Google Generation:

> Our students have changed radically. Today's students are no longer the people our educational system was designed to teach. Today's students have not just changed incrementally from those of the past . . . A really big discontinuity has taken place. One might even call it a 'singularity' – an event which changes things so fundamentally that there is absolutely no going back. This so-called 'singularity' is the arrival and rapid dissemination of digital technology in the last decades of the 20th century.

From that conclusion we have realized that user requirements are no longer predictable: one size no longer fits all, and it is presumptive for us to tell users what they can have. (That goes for our managers, too, although judging by recent events in public and workplace information services they seem to have less of a problem deciding what the users will get and then telling the LIS managers to implement their decisions.)

Summary

Users will not get everything they want, unless perhaps they have the key to unlock ample funding, but nor will they be content with being told what they can have irrespective of their actual and expressed needs. Dialogue is the way forward, as is involvement. Involving users will increase understanding of the issues and constraints; involving and informing organized users (such as Library Friends and the library committee) may well produce innovative solutions or suggest ways that funding can be raised. So we predict that change will go on being the only constant for some time yet – financial change is inevitable, and it doesn't seem worth wagering against considerable political and technological change in the near future.

Doing without some proper knowledge gathering looks like a real gamble.

4

Great expectations: how LIS professionals can manage and train users

In this chapter we discuss:

➡ how to manage users of the service
➡ levels of expectations
➡ the role of the information professional
➡ user training.

In the previous chapter we took a general look at how the nature of library use has been changing, and in particular the impact of the generation known by labels such as 'Digital Natives', 'Gen-Y' and the 'Google Generation'. Now we examine issues in more depth, looking at the changes in the way this generation uses the services we offer, and the new issues this raises for LIS managers.

Managing users of the service
Access

Libraries have long been used to receiving enquiries by telephone and letter, and to dealing with customers beyond the physical building. The professional judgement of reference staff has ensured that the customer has received the most appropriate material to meet the enquiry based on the customer's request and the amount of detail available to refine the enquiry. This remote form of reference interview has served to identify the most suitable materials where the remote customer has been unable to access or assess it.

The widespread development of e-library services has radically changed this model. Using e-services, customers can now view materials online, and select the most useful publications for their purpose. But they can also bypass professional intervention altogether, and run the risk of failing to find all the available materials, perhaps because of failures of their search strategies, or perhaps because their lack of subject knowledge did not alert them to the absence of particular documents. They may well be unaware of relevant resources that are missing from their electronic repository (including of course those that remain only in print-on-paper format).

Identifying authorized users

In the physical library, authorized customers are identified by a physical token such as a ticket or patron card. This is recognized by the staff and an agreed set of privileges is offered to the patron in accordance with his or her membership. This token also acts as an acceptance by the patron of the rules under which the collection is managed, for example by agreeing to a maximum number of items to be borrowed at a time.

However, in virtual libraries there is no such recognition mechanism. Patrons can use the library without being seen or recognized by staff. There is no way of ensuring that they comply with the regulations of the library or any particular restrictions that may apply to the document that they are using.

In many cases, library software will require the user to provide a password to gain authorized access to the service. For example many universities provide a range of remote services to registered users that are accessed over the internet through a login procedure (which may require entry of a password, a physical key such as a chip card inserted in a reader, or the presence of a cookie on the user's computer). Once this is accepted, users can use the library OPAC, and order books and other materials to be delivered. There is also an extensive range of electronic resources including guides to web resources.

Web technology can provide much of the security required, but the solution must allow for those customers who will not (or, on many corporate networks, cannot) comply with the library server's security requirements, such as the use of cookies or security routines activated through particular scripts such as JavaScript or ActiveX. This may become an important issue where there the notion of payment exists; examples would be where services are funded from course fees at educational institutions, or from council tax such as access to electronic reference sources using a public library card number as the login and password. In this area it will improve customer perception if as many obstacles to access as possible can be removed while maintaining security.

Intermediation to support information service users

Remote customers are likely to bypass the library where they have direct access to primary sources and believe, rightly or not, that they possess the skills to retrieve all the information relevant to an enquiry. Indeed, many may do this even without primary sources, and will base their actions and understanding on whatever is in secondary sources (of varying quality!)

Customers who visit the information centre expect to obtain support in the use not only of information but of the technology that presents it. This is one of the issues that supporters of the information commons concept believe is well handled by these new centres (Beatty and White, 2005).

Precisely because they have taken the time to come to the centre these customers will have some expectations, and these will be higher still if they have come because they want to use a product that cannot be networked beyond the campus (however defined in your instance). But we are sure that most library and information professionals would want to provide that kind of support to their on-site users, and that it might well become a selling point for the service if users knew that they can get professional help.

In our view the increasingly widespread use of electronic

information resources has the potential to increase the value of professional intermediation. The information service can relegate low-level enquiries to be resolved by customer use of web-based and other electronic services, making time and room for higher value interaction and more complex research by information staff. However, this higher value and more focused service provision needs to be pointed out both to users (who may become less aware over time of the support that is available) and to business managers who may continue with the line that professional intermediation is unnecessary where universal web access is available.

It needs to be understood by customers (and the financial managers) that it is an important professional skill to handle more complex enquiries and to know when to switch from free resources to professional online services. In an environment where there is no obvious guide to the reliability and quality of information resources accessible to LIS customers, identifying and certifying the quality of electronic sources is essential. Recent experience suggests that there may be issues about the reliability of internal services and their quality control processes, while users are faced with a plethora of external websites with no guide to their information management standards. (In both these cases we are thinking as much of the way that sites retain subscriber data as of the accuracy of their content.) The LIS should consider whether some kind of certification system would address these issues – applying a label of quality to reliable external services might establish a certificate that internal database owners would also be pleased to bid for.

We will discuss the role of the information professional again later in this chapter.

Keeping existing customers

Electronic services give libraries and information centres the chance to expand their clientele and improve their service to existing customers with relatively little effort. Service improvements are possible, for example by providing additional access to materials in demand by appropriate licensing of electronic copies rather than depending on single copies in a fixed geographic location such as a short loan collection. Additional customers can be given access to the collection – although that may mean that existing customers perceive a decline in the quality of the service they receive as new users make demands and reduce the 'spare' time available in the system for more leisurely and possibly more attentive service to those existing users.

But technological development continues to be very rapid. Users may have higher quality technology on their desk than the library and therefore consider it to be technologically backward. Unless the debacle of the Domesday Disc is to be repeated (Darlington, Finney and Pearce, 2003), libraries may well need to retain superseded technology to maintain access to older products, which may well be justified, so the information service needs to explain these reasons, and to demonstrate that it also has access to the latest advances. This is a complicated trick that is likely to make use of currently fashionable technology (such as social networking through Facebook, Twitter and LinkedIn – or their successors) and will need the information service team to make judgements about what has become permanent and useful, and what is interesting but transitory.

So keeping customers may be difficult: faced with this kind of choice, users may decide to bypass the library altogether and use other routes to information. Keeping older machines for use with less technically advanced products involves costs – spares are becoming rarer, as are working old machines that can be cannibalized – so a convincing business case must be made for the investment. On a practical note, space must be found for the growing pool of computers of different vintages.

Some players in the information market have realized that here lie opportunities for them. They are developing business models that give end-users direct access to information that was previously only available in libraries. e-brary (www.ebrary.com) is one such supplier, allowing users to search its range of books and pamphlets, and purchase copies of sections (using the copy function of the web browser) for a few cents, or to print out a few pages. Access is through a user interface that alters the configuration of the browser and allows the user to unlock security settings on the documents displayed in return for the appropriate sum. Payment is from an account set up using a credit card. Although e-brary targets librarians as one of its major user communities and promotes its subscription/ownership model as a benefit to library resource managers, the service is also targeted at corporate users where users in subscribing organizations can find quantities of information without professional involvement.

So there are choices to be made and librarians need to decide which services to concentrate on. It may be reasonable for library users to use electronic services such as e-brary for simple retrieval tasks, and the information professionals would most effectively concentrate on ensuring that existing customers continue to use the library for their more complex enquiries. The mistake would be to try to compete with commercial information services, which are funded on commercial lines and will eventually fail or succeed on that basis, rather than using the time and resource to deal with perceived or actual problems in the library service that are reported by users.

From the library viewpoint, it is worth observing that a single electronic version of a document available from an online vendor will not be sufficient for all the potential users of the library. For example different editions of Shakespeare are needed by doctoral researchers and A-level students, and a single online edition is unlikely to fit all sizes.

The library will use its energies best by explaining this to users and offering a range of alternatives. Patrons will be more likely to remain good users of an LIS that is visibly dealing with the issues that make the electronic alternatives attractive.

Inducements to desert

A number of reasons have been identified that may make existing users more likely to rely on external electronic services, and some of them are entirely valid. Research shows, for example, that in many libraries the OPAC is difficult to use and the information that it contains is frequently incomplete.

In one observed case a noted scientist complained that he would need to travel to Michigan from Europe in order to view a French mathematical treatise from the early 1970s. In the event there were copies in several university libraries in Paris, but their OPACs were unable to provide the search facilities needed to locate the document (Jacquesson, 2000).

Paradoxically, the complexity of digital library interfaces in the library may make customers more likely to desert to a single but incomplete alternative.

In another study, this time in the USA, a librarian found that physicists were going to a local e-print repository for information rather than using the more comprehensive INSPEC service. But there was a sting in the tail: although the scientists were missing out on a considerable area of literature because they were only accessing what was present in the archive, it was found that they were getting far superior current awareness because of the time delay in indexing literature in the e-print archive. One solution here would clearly have been to improve current awareness while at the same time making the INSPEC service better known and more widely available.

This message is increasingly being heard. In the legal field, free legal resource aggregators are building websites that provide services that almost match the paid-for suppliers. An important question for the librarians in this field is how they will demonstrate to users that the advantage in using the library and its paid-for services remains sufficient for them to remain faithful.

Keeping customers: what works

The bottom line seems clear enough: you can keep existing customers when you expand your e-service, but it takes effort. A number of e-suppliers are on the side of the librarian, principally the periodicals agents or book jobbers who have developed e-services with the support of and through supporting the information profession; but a number of new style web-based suppliers have more commercial motives and do not form part of this shared tradition.

Above all, make it easy for the customer. (Ranganathan's dictum holds true – save the time of the reader.) Customers for your e-service are not using it to be impressed by your adherence to technical standards. They come to you because they have a paper to write by the end of the week, or because they need to know the location of a particular document.

The implications of opening up your services

You might well decide that there are advantages in opening up your services to a wider audience – for example, promotion of your organization or community, collaboration with the information services run by related groups, or to achieve more even distribution of demand. But there is a balance to be struck, and the decision to offer widespread access to your service is not only a financial one. Clearly there will be direct costs in staff and technical resources, but there may be indirect costs (or benefits) in terms of reputation and the management of expectations.

Levels of user expectations

User expectations may be difficult to manage when some of those users are located in an organization outside the libraries' parent body. In the special library sector, there may be questions of commercial sensitivity that would make it more difficult to provide external services. In the education sector, there are potential problems with licensing, which may make it difficult to provide a service to users located outside the physical boundaries of the institution. The rules controlling local government finance may make it more difficult to provide services to people who do not live, study or work in the local authority area. But these are becoming real issues for the library and information community, and previous assumptions about service provision are being challenged by new delivery models such as the growth in the number of cultural trusts.

Taking on new customers may be a risky move if, in order to serve them, you have to reduce the quality of service to your existing customers. Nevertheless, the evidence suggests that you may need to find new customers to maintain a visible level of use that equates to present levels, because fewer people are likely to visit the physical collections of your library. Traditional counting of library activities (in particular visits and loan transactions) no longer provides a true picture of the levels of use; but it may be difficult to convince non-librarian managers of this.

Web monitoring software will provide information about the users of your electronic services that includes their identity and navigation patterns, showing you whether you have an important number of external users and whether they are seeking information that is significantly different from what your 'home' users look for. It will highlight issues such as whether you have a particular resource that external users visit you (virtually) to consult, and thus whether you have a resource not widely available elsewhere. The point of course is that your internal users may experience poorer service if that resource experiences heavy demand from elsewhere.

If however you are satisfied that taking on new customers is a sensible move, then you should seek those users. If those new customers are external then setting up connection to you is their responsibility not yours, and you can focus on identifying and adding content to your service rather than becoming bogged down in technical issues. But of course you will still need to provide support to users within your primary customer group.

Service to external users does not have to consist solely, or indeed at all, of the supply of electronic documents taken from the library's collection. The technical facilities that are readily available allow services to external customers to be delivered by e-mail, telephone or streaming media. The standard Microsoft office desktop has facilities that can enable real-time interaction between user and information professional and libraries are using such technologies.

Social media have a role to play here. The simplest introduction is to accept SMS messages renewing or requesting library materials, a fairly widespread facility in Finland, where 'researchers have computers and students have mobile phones' (Pasenen and Muhonen, 2002); but there is increasing expectation that information services will make use of new social media to deliver and promote their services (Bradley, 2007). These include libraries in Second Life (see Alliance Virtual Library, http://infoisland.org for further information); promotional and how-to items on YouTube (for example the University of Wales Institute, Cardiff induction video at www.youtube.com/watch?v=OSPTvcuZTv); and presences on Facebook and Twitter. By the time you have this book in your hands there will doubtless be further 'must-be-there' services to be evaluated in the context of information service delivery.

Licensing arrangements will affect what you can make available beyond the physical limits of your organization's premises and you may be contractually prevented from offering some parts of the collection to external users. (And do be aware that there are different ways of defining your premises, especially where your organization is housed in several buildings. Even if these buildings are next door to one another, if there are public roads between them your supplier may count them as multiple separate locations.) At the same time you will have to recognize those areas where your collection is seen as a leader in the field, and where there is thus an expectation that it might be made more widely available. Licensing conditions may also prevent you from selling the service, and there may also be copyright constraints. In the latter case these will vary from country to country, and we recommend that you take competent legal advice if you are considering taking on customers from outside your own country and providing them with e-services. Make sure that your adviser is conversant with copyright and intellectual property, and, preferably, understands the international as well as the domestic issues raised.

The role of the information professional in delivering customer services

Introducing electronic services brings new professional skills into play. If you are the manager of an electronic service, your staff must have the required abilities to help and deal with the users' needs. It will be important that others (users and non-LIS professional managers) are aware of the range of skills, since it may appear that the work is being deskilled by the increased use of external information sources.

Delivering what customers want goes beyond simply being good at providing service – which is essentially what a successful retail business must also do. So what distinguishes a professional service and the role of the information professional in delivering it? The Special Libraries Association addressed this question in its report *Competencies for Information Professionals of the 21st Century* (2003):

An Information Professional ('IP') strategically uses information in his/her job to advance the mission of the organization. The IP accomplishes this through the development, deployment, and management of information resources and services. The IP harnesses technology as a critical tool to accomplish goals. IPs include, but are not limited to librarians, knowledge managers, chief information officers, web developers, information brokers, and consultants.

In the information and knowledge age, specialists in information management are essential – they provide the competitive edge for the knowledge-based organization by responding with a sense of urgency to critical information needs. Information, both internally and externally produced, is the lifeblood of the knowledge-based organization and essential for innovation and continuing learning. Information sharing is also essential for any organization that is attempting to understand and manage its intellectual capital, often in a global context. IPs play a unique role in gathering, organizing and coordinating access to the best available information sources for the organization as a whole. They are also leaders in devising and implementing standards for the ethical and appropriate use of information.

If IPs did not exist they would be reinvented as organizations struggle to gain control over ever-increasing amounts of information in multiple storage formats. The astounding growth of the Internet and the rise of electronic communications and storage media generally have transformed our work and personal lives. Information overload is a growing problem and IPs are needed more than ever to quality filter and provide needed information in an actionable form.

The report goes on to say that in order to fulfil their purpose, information professionals require various competencies – professional, personal and core competencies that anchor the professional and personal competencies.

This seems an excellent summary that would be hard to better. In the context we have been discussing, information professionals are doing excellent but undervalued work such as:

- evaluating services and certifying the quality of websites
- providing support and training for people using networked e-services
- continuing the higher-value paid-for reference and search services that are not replaced by the new offerings
- finding new resources for the network
- understanding of the search process and the improved quality their intervention can provide
- adding metadata to site links and e-documents so that retrieval becomes easier and hits are more relevant
- making the electronic services easier to use than the suppliers have done.

Training

With so much rapid development going on, it is important that information professionals stay at the leading edge, and also that users of the service are able to take fullest advantage (and the most economical advantage) of what is on offer. This means two things: training and awareness.

For many practitioners the best training is likely to include participation at conferences and other exchanges of experience. The highly technical nature of some areas of the work highlights the need for specialist workshops as well as more general awareness sessions. But the opportunities offered by social media has brought many informal channels through blogs and other forms of commentary as well as the training available in media such as YouTube and Second Life.

Front-line support staff will need a different kind of training, to ensure that they can talk users through the service both for initial understanding and to resolve any later problems. Helpdesk skills will be important where few customers visit the library but rely on e-mail or telephone contact to resolve problems.

New forms of service delivery will demand wider skills than in the traditional library and this may need to be picked up in formal training programmes. Technical staff need to acquire basic library skills including simple enquiry work, while librarians need to have basic technical skills that will allow service to continue out of standard working hours, reflecting the convergence of functions found in the information commons approach.

User training

As we mentioned earlier, many users of the service will need to understand the changes that have taken place in the service. Areas such as copyright and intellectual property will need particular attention, as it is here that problems can unintentionally arise. Even where, as with the recent changes in Australian copyright law, the onus is on the external user to comply with the law rather more than it is on the library providing the service, it is vital that users understand their obligations and do not inadvertently fall foul of the rules.

A training statement should form part of the plan for introducing electronic information services. It should cover staff, users and the management structure within which the information and library service is located. It may be appropriate to include presentations to the board of directors, academic board or council of your organization in this statement. The statement will cover library and information professional, technical and communications training, and include details of any training of trainers that may be required, for example in preparation for a cascaded introduction of the e-service. Do not underestimate the resources needed for this work, either in terms of the cost of training, or (as has emerged from the introduction of the People's Network in the UK's public libraries – www.peoplesnetwork.gov.uk) to cover the essential work of those being trained.

What do we really know about user needs and behaviour?

Taking care of users is an essential part of the information professional's daily tasks. 'It costs five times as much to attract a new customer as it does to keep an existing one', according to Norman Scarborough, assistant professor of economics and business administration at Presbyterian College in Clinton, SC, USA. 'It's also smart marketing to reach out to someone who has already been a customer in the past. That's an easy sale' (Zimmerer, Scarborough and Wilson, 2007).

So are the answers to these questions already available within your community? Can you answer the following questions:

- Who on the LIS staff really knows the users?
- What percentage of the total user population do they know about?
- Is time allocated so that LIS staff can talk to customers?
- Are any surveys carried out, or any feedback forms available on the LIS website?
- Are users informed of any new services? If so is there any follow-up to ascertain what the user thought about this information or about the actual services?
- Do you stay in touch with the users? (Don't let customers go too long without thinking of your LIS. There is an increasing range of means to get your message across, from traditional direct mail, through e-mail alerts, to new approaches such as Twitter and Facebook groups.)

- What are your unique selling points (USPs) as an information service – and how do the users perceive them? What can you give your users that they cannot get anywhere else? We know for example the electronic services OSH UPDATE (www.oshupdate.com) and FIREINF (www.fireinf.com) are unique collections of health, safety and fire information that they cannot be obtained from other sources.

When you run a training seminar or provide a new service, follow up with delegates and users to find out what they think about them. That way, if they are happy, you can ask for referrals. If they are not, you are the first to know and have a chance to set things right.

Give your users superior service and convenience. Many are so busy that they are willing to pay for extra convenience; you should emphasize the value of your services in providing that convenience.

Find out what users want and within the constraints of cost and priorities aim to provide it. You can give users more than they expect at little or no cost, for example by spending a few extra minutes helping a user solve a problem or researching a new topic in order to become the community's expert. By giving the users more than they believe they have paid for, your LIS will become an indispensible element in your organization or community.

Summary

At first glance it might appear obvious who the users of a library and information service are; closer examination shows that this is not such a simple question. Every service is different for a variety of political, social and commercial reasons, but for every one of them it's essential to identify the target audience and to define who is a legitimate user of the service.

The questions we have discussed in this and the previous chapter and the sources we have referred to will provide the material to compile a checklist to help to define both the identity and locations of your users. They will also have suggested other issues that you may want to explore, particularly if providing electronic resources has created a new and distinct audience for your service. And your research may also have suggested ways in which new users can be attracted (together with their funding, we hope) and areas where your staff and users will need to develop their skills to take fullest advantage of your investment in information resources.

5

Using information about past user behaviour

In this chapter we look at:

➡ the value of information about past user behaviour
➡ the content of library surveys, and how this influences the way that users respond
➡ what the results of your information audit may tell you about user needs
➡ how to use the results of surveys to adjust services
➡ how to use the results of surveys to decide whether to close services or create new ones
➡ the value of information over time.

The value of information about past user behaviour

What information do you already hold about your users and what can you learn from it? Past behaviour is no guarantee of future behaviour, of course, so is it worth keeping old data? There may be changes in the size or composition of your user group, and older reviews are unlikely to cover some of the services your LIS now offers, just as they may include some services that have since closed. Historic data will of course allow you to paint a picture over time of how the LIS is used, and how users regard it and its services, allowing you to track trends and comparative figures to support business cases and help with fund allocation. But there is also great value in reading the detail, because of what it tells you about the way that users have interpreted the questions put to them. You may be able not only to identify areas where jargon or lack of understanding is confusing your users (and maybe dissuading them from asking the LIS to provide a new service you would like to offer) but also gain understanding about the way that your users work and how they involve the LIS in that work.

An important byproduct of reviewing what you already know will be to highlight other information stores in your organization, and this may lead you to consider whether these should be brought within your library and information service, or whether you should influence their management in any other appropriate ways.

Library surveys

Do you issue library surveys? Many libraries do, not only to discover what users require, but in order to decide what services to provide and in order to allocate budgets to them. Surveys are however a two-edged sword. Although they can be helpful in indicating users' reaction to and valuation of the services that you ask about, they may not elicit helpful information about things you do not mention in the survey. In other words, you have to depend on your users mentioning things that you forget to ask about. If you now bear in mind the well known effect of 'survey fatigue' (which means it's a bad idea to issue supplementary surveys to cover the questions you forgot) then you will realize how important it is to ask the right questions first time, because you are unlikely to get a further chance for some months to come.

What do you ask in your surveys?

There is sound advice available on how to compile a survey, both in general (Accesscable.net, 1997; Sue and Ritter, 2007; Dillman et al., 2008; TechSoup, 2008) and specifically for LIS (Library Research Service, 2003). The choice of questions is important: ask too many and users are deterred from completing the survey; ask too few and you end up without all the information that you need to plan the service.

But have you considered the type of question that needs to be asked and answered? Many library surveys ask about existing services: but it is too easy to include questions that may be difficult for users to answer meaningfully.

Here is a real example – 'The following are databases to be used only at the Library: check any you have used in the past year. FirstSearch (OCLC). . . . EBSCOhost Magazine Index . . . Medline Plus.' Will enough respondents know that they used FirstSearch as an intermediary to ERIC, or the difference between Medline in FirstSearch and Medline Plus to give an accurate and therefore helpful response? (Will they even know what is in each of these databases?) And do questions like these allow people to tell you that they had problems finding anything useful to meet their information needs?

Of particular interest are the questions that ask users to make selections from a list, for example to rank services or to arrange a list of future priorities in order of preference: 'What are YOUR top priorities for the library in the next two years? Tick up to five', says one example, which is followed by a list of topics identified by the library. If there is no space for free text these, like other closed questions, deter users from expressing their real requirements. And if the library tells its users which priorities they can choose from, then it looks as if there wasn't really any choice in the first place.

How information audits can help

Chapter 2 discusses the value of information auditing and reminds you that we have provided fuller details of this technique in other publications. But it's worth taking a look at the potential of information audits to provide a lot of answers about past behaviour that will help you to give future LIS users what they want.

Information auditing seeks to discover what information resources are needed by people within an organization to carry out their tasks (which can mean anything from CEOs using corporate information services in a multinational company to members of the public looking for a book on growing roses); where those resources are in the organization (easier to capture and describe in a public library, but still not 100% simple); and how access works or what restrictions there are (resource sharing, closed access, etc.). In the model we have developed we consider issues such as whether there are duplicate collections and whether wider use can be made of the information available, and we challenge user behaviour where it equates to 'information is power' leading to unwarranted retention and restriction of information that has justified wider use.

We use checklists and questionnaires to discover the existence of relevant resources, and to explore the use being made of them. An information audit provides the organization with a wealth of important data such as:

- what information exists within the organization
- where it is located
- how many sections within the organization or the community being served have their own collections of information, or have an official branch of the information service
- what information the organization needs and when it is needed
- who uses it
- what gaps exist
- where potential customers for information are in the organization
- why people use a particular service or source of information in preference to others
- why some people use the service frequently and some just occasionally
- why some people never use the service
- how to produce the information in the format needed
- what training is needed for staff and users.

The information obtained through surveys should be supplemented by discussions with managers or other representatives of your user group so that you can gather details of the types of information that your user community needs. The outcome of the exercise should be a clearer understanding of the ways that users currently access information, and of the types of information that they use.

If it turns out that users are not making use of resources in the way that information managers expect it is important to enquire further to find out why. For example, the information audit may show requirements for some kinds of information that are not currently available in the organization and where users are going without important data or are going outside to obtain it. The audit question-naire will also identify specialist information needs together with systems and services that your potential clients are using to meet those requirements. Our books *Creating a Successful E-Information Service* (Pantry and Griffiths, 2002); *Developing a Successful Service Plan* (Pantry and Griffiths, 2000); and *Becoming a Successful Intrapreneur* (Pantry and Griffiths, 1998) explain these ideas in more detail.

What the results of your information audit may tell you about user needs
Users in search of information that you don't hold

Not long ago users had few choices available when they were unable to obtain required information from the libraries that they had access to. Often these choices entailed extensive bibliographic research and possibly the need to convince information gatekeepers that the cost was justified of obtaining this information from national repositories. The result was that users went without, and the library may well have incurred costs in initial research and communicating with the user to see whether an alternative requirement could be established.

The internet and electronic journals have changed all that. Especially if they have an Athens password it is possible for your users to access electronic journals from many locations. They can find many articles on the web (not always legally, it's true, and some users have a hazy understanding of their 'right' to use passwords after they have left an educational institution) and they can readily read abstracts of articles and books on the websites of external aggregators such as Emerald and Ingenta as well as e-journal suppliers such as Swets and Ebsco.

So, potential users can bypass your library or information service unless you make it so valuable that they cannot do without it. This requires a combination of excellent service (for customer delight) and what might be best summarized as user education in information literacy. We talked earlier about the fallacy that everything is available on the internet, and is free. Engaging with potential users who see no reason to become actual users requires fallacies such as this to be successfully challenged.

Non-users in search of information somewhere else

Let's break it down a little more. First, non-users frequently assume that your service cannot provide the answers they require. This may be through ignorance of what your service can offer; it may be because the user tried (tested) you before and thought your service fell short of expectations; or it may be because the user consulted your catalogue or e-journals collection and couldn't find what they thought they needed. The user may believe that they have specialist understanding of the subject that is not shared by the LIS staff and therefore the information need is taken to an external supplier. All of these behaviours must be tackled and resolved.

Second, there's the belief that everything that's known is on the internet, and for free. We quoted a couple of comments on this 'Google fallacy' earlier, and we set out our view in Chapter 1 of *Setting up a Library and Information Service from Scratch* (Pantry and Griffiths, 2005) where we said:

Information is after all widespread and pervasive. There is certainly more information in existence than at any time in history (by definition, when you think about it), but more than that it is increasing in quantity at a faster and faster rate. Estimates suggest it is doubling in little more than two years, and that people today can acquire more knowledge in a day than was known in a lifetime by people little more than a hundred years ago. Along with the pervasiveness of information, the view seems to be increasing that managing this information and knowledge is a skill that takes no special ability or training, and that there is no problem in dealing with this mass of detail provided that this or that software is purchased and put to work on the organization's intranet. Not only this, the argument goes on, but there is at least one page on the internet where somebody has put all that anyone needs to know on any important subject, and that page is accurate, reliable, authoritative and timely – and available free of charge as the internet represents a kind of information-based virtual philanthropic institution. All such pages are flawlessly indexed by Google (for there is no other search engine), which can be relied on to place them at the top of the list of items retrieved no matter which term or synonym is entered. So it follows that there is no need for any information service in any organization or community, because now that internet access is universal all anyone needs to do is to navigate to Google and use the results to inform their business, social and educational decisions and opinions.

Somehow, we don't think so. The problem of course is that when the argument is set out like this an information professional recognizes at once how shallow and inaccurate it is – yet many people who are responsible for organizations or communities actually think like this. So you may have some work to do to convince the person or people who put you onto the creation of an information service that this is a serious job, and if that person is a convert then you may have to give them the evidence to contradict others who argue against having the information service. The intention of this book is to do this by describing how to create and operate the kind of service that will meet the real information needs of its users, and provide a continuous reminder of the difference that library and information professionals make. In time you will acquire your own stock of stories and anecdotes that illustrate this value within your own community – for the time being you will have to rely on ours!

Clearly there is a problem if you discover either of these problems through your audit, and you may wonder whether you can do anything to tackle them. These are issues where persuasion and demonstration may be the best approaches – though in times of increasing financial pressures it may be simple enough to demonstrate savings. For example, a basic audit in one government office discovered four subscriptions to a database that charged a monthly fee in return for 20 hours use – but each user was consuming only two or three hours a month. A check with the supplier established that there was nothing to prevent them sharing a single password and a 75% saving was quickly made, with spare capacity most months and additional hours purchased singly when a rush of work led to higher demand. Another similar exercise in another organization revealed that newly qualified legal staff were continuing to make use of university passwords to access legal databases – with the result that the university was technically in breach of its contracts and could have been penalized, and the opportunity to provide useful databases for the entire cadre of lawyers was being lost because the usage was not visible to the LIS.

Using the results of surveys to adjust services

You must act on the results of any surveys that you decide to undertake. It is annoying for your users if you collect data that appears to have no purpose or effect, and they likely to be less co-operative if you appear to be collecting data for its own sake. As happened in one survey we observed, more users commented on the fact that four pages had been stapled in upside down than any other question with a write-in box; and we suspect that was because the users were accustomed to the annual survey being followed by little or no action based on the results.

Action is not always possible at once; you may for example have to wait for renewal time in order to adjust subscriptions to journals and e-journals. That needs to be explained to users, but negotiations should begin with suppliers as soon as a new or substantially amended requirement is established that you have decided to meet.

Using the results of surveys to decide whether to close services or create new ones

How good was your survey form? And did you ask the right questions in your one to one interviews with key users and non-users? The answers to these questions will be evident from the results of your surveys and what they tell you. The information needs of communities, businesses and education change over time: new subjects and concerns become important, technological change brings new topics of research, and population shifts can alter the make-up of your user group and therefore the languages and types of information they need. Add these results to your own horizon scanning and current awareness searches (which need only be in the form of a few key phrases scanned by Google Alerts, or can be full-blown stored searches on professional databases) and you should begin to see a picture of what are likely to be the current and future information requirements (or interests) of your community.

Closing services is never popular with their users, but the time comes when the investment of resources is not being paid back as benefit. If your survey shows that people no longer need a particular service, or want it delivered in a new way, then that becomes your priority rather than propping up a declining service. Just as music libraries no longer keep stock of eight-track cartridges (see http://en.wikipedia.org/wiki/Stereo_8) because that technology went out of common use around 1980, so you need to decide when services or activities have reached their sell-by date based on what the survey results are telling you. That releases the resources that go into new e-journals, setting up a Twitter feed, SMS messages to remind people when items are due for return, and so on.

Our key messages are, first, that having carried out surveys and audits, you must act on those findings that send a clear message about your users' requirements and expectations; and second, that communications are as always important – those people losing a service they value will need to be reassured that there are sound reasons for the change, and that you will do your best to provide a viable alternative.

The value of information over time

Finally, as we have said constantly, no survey or audit stands alone. Keep the results of your enquiries, and return to them over time to see trends. Go back to your users – if you identify them by role as well as name you will still get meaningful results even if key members of your user community move on – and ask them for updated information at intervals. Include new questions about obvious trends, and take out questions about services that have been discontinued (obvious, yes, but easy to forget to do). Taken with other data such as that delivered by your library management system, you should be able to demonstrate the changes in your user community, the way it uses your service, and their expectations. Other documents such as committee minutes and business cases will provide the rest of the detail to show how you managed the service in order to provide your users with the best possible quality for the available resources. Bear in mind that you may know all this detail but you are also likely to move on, and your successor may have to learn what you already know from long experience. If possible, mark the records for longer-term retention or keep a basic set of findings as part of the LIS manager's working papers – by its very nature this kind of data needs more than short-term retention and must not be seen as merely ephemeral.

Case study: UK government libraries

The Committee of Departmental Librarians (CDL), which is the management committee for UK government department libraries, compiles an annual series of statistics of use that aggregates use across all departments. The results were incorporated into the long-running LISU Annual Library Statistics series; the volume covering 2006 figures (Creaser, Maynard and White, 2007) was the last as the series was discontinued due to lack of funding. Table 5.1, extracted from the figures provided by CDL, shows clearly how from 1993–4 to 2003–4 the number of enquiries and loans handled by government libraries declined substantially while online searches increased. But the number of items catalogued remained fairly constant, while at the end of the period the number of online searches seemed to be levelling out, probably because of the growth of the 'Google factor' around that time. (But do not jump to rigid conclusions – the number of libraries providing figures fell by 50% or more in some categories, and there is no indicator showing how the type of enquiries handled might have changed over ten years.) What conclusions would you reach about placing resources, for example on enquiry desks rather than cataloguing teams?

Table 5.1 Extract of UK government library statistics 1993–4 to 2003–4

Year	Enquiries	Loans	Searches	Total staff	Libraries
1993-4	1,017,691	2,601,173	42,060	698	59
1994-5	767,457	1,312,072	55,754	642	44
1995-6	797,582	1,331,770	69,339	635	45
1996-7	682,770	1,017,572	86,499	631	50
1997-8	1,053,783	1,232,750	106,694	737	45
1998-9	558,295	339,375	136,462	524	29
1999-2000	623,404	1,148,265	155,336	769	32
2000-1	504,571	1,020,881	134,259	760	33
2001-2	283,633	136,129	36,538	472	22
2002-3	280,085	133,765	87,654	531	23
2003-4	146,949	82,517	n/a	305	18

Of course there are other background issues you would need to know about in order to make full use of these figures – such as dates of elections, changes in departmental responsibilities and any major research initiatives – but these extracts are sufficient to give you some idea of the value of collecting data over a period of time. (So it is unfortunate that the LISU compendium is no longer published although of course all the contributors go on collecting local data for their own use.) You can also see the effect of gaps in data collection, and how failure to make allowances for this could lead you to false conclusions.

Summary

This chapter has looked in depth at the value of information already available and how to combine it with other information such as current awareness to derive intelligence that will help you to manage your LIS. Use the techniques of information auditing to find out more about your own information needs as well as those of your user community!

6

Making the most of knowing your users

This chapter looks at how you can improve your strategic planning through analysis of user behaviour by:

➡ making the link to strategic planning
➡ better marketing
➡ keeping the customers satisfied
➡ keeping upstream management satisfied
➡ making sure that your organization recognizes the importance of its library and information service
➡ communications
➡ achieving cost benefits and making better use of budgets.

Better strategic planning through analysis of user behaviour

Library and information services do not operate in 'steady state'. They are – or should be – central to every organization irrespective of the field of activity (or 'sector' – by which we mean categories like academic, governmental, workplace, public, legal, financial, technical, scientific or medical). In order to remain in that central role they need constantly to be assessed, evaluated and monitored.

Making the link to strategic planning

It will be part of your strategic planning processes for the LIS to check for and evaluate the many new and competing services and products that constantly arrive on the scene. You should recognize that this is also part of your organization's strategic planning process, so user requirements should be kept in mind as part of your planning and evaluation processes. How can this be done?

Marketing is one way (and we discuss this in a moment) but it's also important to make the leaders of your user community aware of the assumptions or decisions you have made, and to share the information with them. This can be done succinctly – you have no need to go into every detail. In this way you can be sure that these decision makers have a summary of your evidence in front of them, and could ask for further information about particular issues of concern.

It is not among the main aims of this book to provide detailed guidance on the processes of strategic planning for libraries but there are a number of texts that provide further information (such as Corrall 2000 and 2003 or the documents on the web indexed from LibrarySupportStaff.com at www.librarysupportstaff.com/strategicplan. html).

However the pace of change has been rapid in recent years. An indication of the effect of this rapid change is given in the CIBER briefing paper *Information Behaviour of the Researcher of the Future* (2008), which suggests that managers should be

> introducing robust, fit-for-purpose mechanisms for monitoring and evaluating their users (and information services). Faced with the prospect that the future scholar will only ever want to use them remotely it is absolutely crucial that libraries have a means of monitoring and evaluating what they do. Furthermore, it is not sufficient to just listen and monitor it is also necessary to change in response to this data. Otherwise libraries will be increasingly marginalized and anonymized in the virtual information world. No private sector corporation would survive on the basis of failing to invest in consumer profiling, market research and loyalty programmes.

No library we are aware of has a department devoted to the evaluation of the user, how can that be?

The same report further advises that strategic management requires

> really getting information skills on the agenda because clearly people are having great difficulties navigating and profitting from the virtual scholarly environment. To succeed it will be necessary to lead on outcomes/benefits (better researchers, degrees etc) and work closely with publishers.
>
> We in the information and library profession need to take action for our own profession because . . . the library profession desperately needs leadership to develop a new vision for the 21st century and reverse its declining profile and influence. This should start with effecting that shift from a content-orientation to a user-facing perspective and then on to an outcome focus.

In another study, Lennart Björneborn, Royal School of Library and Information Science, Copenhagen, in the working paper *Libraries as Integrative Interfaces – tracking users' information interaction in context* (2006), outlines an ongoing exploratory research project concerned with how users interact with the physical interior of public libraries. The project focuses especially on how users combine purposeful, goal-directed information behaviour with more divergent behaviour like explorative browsing and serendipity to find interesting materials in the library. The project uses several methods based on those used by research into shopping behaviour such as sweeping whole library sections for 'snapshots' of users' activities, tracking traffic routes and user destinations, monitoring selected spots, registering traces of material usage, data mining of circulation statistics, and observing individual users' information behaviour supplemented with interviews and questionnaires. The paper suggests that libraries can be viewed as integrative interfaces that invite users to interact with the diversity of human, physical and digital information resources available in the library.

Better marketing

Marketing is an important tool that influences user behaviour in library and information services. Equally, user behaviour and your observation of it should influence the ways that you market your library and information service. A moment's reflection will make it clear that it is wasted effort to promote a service that is already operating to capacity, and that successful marketing in this case may result in unwelcome budget pressures. Observing and measuring user behaviour, particularly using methods that interact with users (such as surveys or focus groups), may indicate whether high levels of use indicate truly popular services or those that are heavily used as the nearest available thing to the real requirement, which has yet to be expressed and fulfilled. In a case study of strategic management in a UK government library service (Taylor and Corrall, 2007) one of the key findings was the need for improved strategic marketing. Among the methods proposed were building a strong brand to reclaim information territory, promoting information needs assessments to target groups, getting involved in business and project planning, communicating the services offered and policy on charging, exploiting customer relationship management tools and techniques, and using established channels of communication (e.g. meetings and e-mail).

Singh (2009a) identifies a strong correlation between the degree of marketing and library performance. He highlights the need to align library service and performance to customer expectations, moving customers' view of the library from 'them-and-us' to 'we'. He develops these ideas further in a second article (2009b) to segment libraries' marketing attitudes, knowledge and behaviour, again concluding that based on studies among Finnish research libraries, 'it pays to be market-oriented, the ultimate result being higher customer satisfaction'. And although Hildebrand (2003) is primarily concerned with public library websites, he indicates that delivering electronic services to meet customer expectations may require librarians to take other actions such as re-claiming management of their website from the IT departments that were given control of it while the librarians were otherwise occupied with online catalogues and library management systems issues. Improving service will also require answers to questions of finance and staff management.

Keeping the customers satisfied

Here is a problem during an economic downturn; customers expect continually enhanced service, or at least no worsening of quality, while costs continue to rise and budgets are decreased. In these circumstances it is difficult but necessary to keep customers satisfied and believing that they are receiving the best possible quality service.

Authors such as Chim (2007) remark on increased competition for resources among academic institutions and its effect on their libraries; this seems to us to apply to many kinds of information services at present. In Chim's case (at the Polytechnic University of Hong Kong), the solutions to the problem of maintaining customer satisfaction with reduced resources included a number of recognized techniques such as the Balanced Scorecard, customer surveys, regular meetings with students and lecturers (representing two major customer groups) and benchmarking.

The library may of course already be keeping its customers satisfied, but with the problems that either the customers do not recognize that it's the library that gives them that satisfaction (Connaway et al., 2008) or that the customers are paying someone else to provide them with what the community's library service is already providing free of charge for its members (Williams, 2006).

There is growing evidence that user behaviour has been changed by the rapid development of electronic document collections. The observations by Dempsey (2008, 2009) have already been noted concerning users' reluctance to use materials that do not fit their primary requirements in terms of format or accessibility: a number of the authors listed here remark on students' expectations to be able to access library materials on their own electronic devices, and to share materials regardless of copyright and other restrictions – both of which pose obvious problems for libraries in terms of IT networking, document formats and intellectual property management.

Others have commented on the rapid growth of social networking websites and highlight the need to communicate with library users, particularly students, in their own environments as these modern patrons (or non-patrons) are unwilling to come to the library and its online presence to make use of its facilities. Meredith Farkas (2007), for example, reflects when discussing the Brooklyn College Library's presence on MySpace:

> While students could obviously find all of this information [about library services] and more at the official [library] website, it might not always be the first place they look when doing research. Despite the wealth of library resources, students often use nonacademic search engines when doing coursework. If these same students browse MySpace while they are doing their homework, then the library functioning in that space might be just the reminder they need to use library resources in their next paper.

A recent Danish study (Kann-Christensen and Andersen, 2009) highlights the need to consider inclusion and diversity issues in assessing user satisfaction and user requirements. In the authors' view the public library of Aarhus was achieving the opposite of its stated intention of recognizing diversity, and point to some potential user groups who feel excluded from society in general. If libraries do not directly address the need for inclusion, they may be considered as closed to those who are not (as the authors put it) invited to its party. Creaser, Davies and Wisdom (2002) discuss similar issues in respect of visually impaired people, who widely report satisfaction with library services but the authors report that some of the people surveyed have ceased using certain services because of difficulties in use.

One further point of concern that rose from an American study (Graham, Faix and Hartman, 2009) leads into our next area of discussion, which is about dealing with upward management. This was that use of social networking may involve additional marketing costs for the purchase of applications on the social networking website, but that these purchases may be unconventional from a corporate purchasing viewpoint and may therefore raise questions when accounts are audited or scrutinized. There is, for example, no tangible asset that can be audited and checked in return for the outlay.

Keeping upstream management satisfied

As well as keeping customers satisfied, LIS managers need to keep their own managers satisfied that the service is being properly managed and run. Unless this upward satisfaction is delivered, the LIS team will find obstacles (sometimes unexpected obstacles) being placed in their way, disrupting their focus on delivering customer satisfaction. Worse perhaps, the upstream managers of the library service may consult directly with users (through a library committee, or through surveys undertaken independently of the library) and use the results of these soundings without either having an understanding of the service or the guidance of the LIS staff to tell them what the results are saying.

The first issue is to reassure financial managers that funding is being spent responsibly, effectively and in accordance with the community's regulatory structure. Although your existing systems may be adequate (and hopefully excellent) in accounting for books and journals, how do they cope with newer forms of information and communication?

We mentioned a moment ago the problems that may be set by your audit systems when you pay for applications on a social networking website; you may be able to devise a way of accounting for them, e.g. by listing a URL as the asset. (This is after all what we have done for the best part of two decades when paying for domain names.) What about staff time? An interesting point is made in a New Zealand context by McIntyre and Nicolle (2008):

> The chief cost to the institution [in using blogging as a library commun-
> ications tool] is staff time, which must be carefully managed if blogs are
> to be kept up to date and their audience maintained. Scanning information
> sources falls well within the regular duties of professional librarians, but
> preparing interesting and eloquent posts takes time. Spam comments are

a nuisance and denying these distasteful and inappropriate comments is a negative use of librarians' time and energy.

Externally and internally, a significant benefit to a library is the searchable archive created by the blog software. This is a valuable knowledge resource which preserves information about an institution and makes it available at point of need.

Their observation about users' spam comments reflects our own views on managing the reputation of the LIS, which we discuss later in this chapter.

Making sure that your organization recognizes the importance of its library and information service

What can you do to make sure that your managers understand what the LIS is doing, and in particular that its actions and decisions are responses to the observed and recorded behaviour of patrons? Here are some thoughts; where others seem to be in agreement with us, we have noted this!

Communication, communication, communication: make sure that your strategic plan (see our title *Developing a Successful Service Plan* (Pantry and Griffiths, 2000) for more details of how to write this) includes clear statements of the importance of meeting customer satisfaction; details of how needs and satisfaction are measured; and details of how service adjustments are made to deal with identified gaps (see for example the two articles by Rajesh Singh cited in this chapter). We look in more detail at communication in a moment.

Explain the obscure, but explain the obvious too: despite our detailed knowledge of Web 2.0, Library 2.0 and Business 2.0, and of all the issues that these shorthand names encompass, it is quite possible that the managers responsible for the LIS overall do not share this knowledge. Even where the head of the LIS sits on a board of directors or an equivalent in academia, there are likely to be members who do not understand the issues and do not see why resources should be used to address what may be transitory fads. So business plans, publicity and other documentation need to explain why these issues matter and what the LIS is doing about users' needs. Those needs are likely, by the way, to include some kind of information literacy outreach work because there are users who are unclear about how the technology works ('timid' users as we have categorized them in our books): techniques like making the library available as a Facebook friend or inviting fans (for example, CILT: the National Centre for Languages in London has a Facebook wall at http://en-gb.facebook. com/pages/London-United-Kingdom/CILT-Resources-Library/ 21925889870#/pages/London-United-Kingdom/CILT-Resources-Library/21925889870?v=wall&viewas=0. University College Dublin (UCD) Library is present on Facebook, Flickr, Twitter and Second Life), using social networking to link users and researchers (see discussion at www.daveyp.com/blog/archives/747), sending Twitter updates to make announcements about the library (see example at http://twitter.com/shefinfocommons/), using Flickr as a publicity tool. For example, www.flickr.com/groups/dayiowalibraries/ shows photos from National Library Day 2008 in Iowa Libraries, and http://countyourblessings.wordpress.com/2006/06/08/flickr-for-a-library-tour/ describes the use of Flickr for a library tour website. The list could be endless, as there are hundreds of examples already in cyberspace and they are being added to daily. What's the business advantage? It is explained by Boran (2008) on the Irish technology blog Silicon Republic:

> In existence since early July, the UCD [University College Dublin] library profile on Facebook is a way for social networking loving students to connect with their college library and interact with it in some useful ways.
>
> Students can check to see if the textbook they want is available by searching through the online catalogue directly from Facebook, as well as grabbing a widget that keeps them up to date on library news alerts. This widget can be embedded in their own Facebook profile, as well as on MySpace, LiveJournal and personal blogs.
>
> I was present at the first-ever lecture held by UCD in Second Life and while the move to Facebook may not be anywhere near as innovative as

this, it certainly does have the capacity to reach many more students and make them feel more part of a college network.

There are other standard additions like the discussion board, which doesn't seem to have been used yet, and a Flickr widget showing some snaps in and around the main library on UCD's Belfield campus.

Plus, if you feel like asking the librarian any questions, there is always the chat application available during regular office hours.

Looking about on Facebook there are several US universities, including Harvard of course (Facebook founder Zuckerberg founded the site while he was a student there), and one thing I am looking forward to seeing from a UCD Facebook presence is a video section like Harvard's one, because some great speakers have passed through its gates.

UCD has also set down its experiences, although in the light of the blog post quoted above (July 2008) it is informative to read in Pan (2007) that:

> Every academic library has to decide where to draw the line on the new technologies. We have so far steered clear of a UCD library presence in Flickr or BEBO – certainly not YouTube! We have tended to feel it inappropriate for a scholarly academic library to get involved in environments that deal largely with inconsequential electronic chatter and leisure – but that perspective could well change as we see how these various social networking options develop. We are aware that other libraries have drawn the line differently and *are* developing content within these environments. Indeed we have been persuaded to take the plunge into one of these social environments. And that is Second Life.

Although financial managers are necessarily hard to satisfy, these arguments suggest that current students have radically different approaches to information access and retrieval that these tools satisfy, while the coming generation of students ('screenagers' as they are increasingly being labelled, 'digital natives' in other terminology) will find it difficult to study in more traditional styles. In other words the argument is truly 'adapt or die'; given the well-known issues with search engine dependence, a move away from the reliable resources in libraries and information services will in the long term be highly detrimental to scholarship and knowledge – although maybe it will throw up some unexpected discoveries along the way! This appears to be an issue of considerable concern in Denmark as several of the Danish-language papers referred to in Lennart Björneborn's work at the Danmarks Biblioteksskole in Copenhagen (see his page at www.db.dk/ombiblioteksskolen/medarbejdere/default.asp?cid=596&tid =4) include discussion of growing dependence on Google. Some suggestions are discussed below:

- Trumpet success: ensure that communications and business plans include a look back to What Worked (or lessons learned from What Didn't), so that it is clear that library management is an active business and not simply maintaining the status quo in a repository that does not continue to meet the community's needs. But do make sure that you take heed of the contents of this section, and that it is not simply window dressing.
- Make reporting clear and structured. Templates such as the submissions used by the UK civil service ensure that issues are presented clearly with all relevant information (financial, environmental, political and so on) identified by headings that also serve as a reminder of the information needed by high level decision makers. Not least, the civil service submission template reminds the writer to start with a summary of the issue, the urgency, and the recommendation for action (Griffiths, 2009).
- Ensure that upstream managers are aware that problems have been spotted and neutralized. Risk registers are one way of doing this; but in less formal documents, at least include a note highlighting drawbacks that have been reported and explain how they will be prevented from happening again in your service. Keeping with the theme of library and Web 2.0 applications in the LIS, show that the potential for negative uses of social media (see for example Camber, 2007) are known and that vigilance will be maintained to stamp out abuse.

Communications

As we have just indicated, communication is an essential part of maintaining customer satisfaction. People need to know what is going on, why it is happening and what is likely to happen afterwards. When the benefits start to be felt, people should be told what has been achieved and left in no doubt that this is down to the work done by the library and information service. There need to be positive incentives for people to switch to your new ways of doing things, and one good way of doing this is to tell them about the successes that they could be part of.

> Communication was seen as paramount as we firmly believed that better communication within the Libraries and between the Libraries and its user community should result in better customer service levels. We undertook several surveys in order to assess how staff perceived communication both internally and externally and how it might be improved.
>
> (Sidorko and Yang, 2009)

What new items of information has your work created? These could be, for example:

- descriptive documents setting out the way information is managed in the community
- statements of information requirements around the organization, which could be shared with those just starting to define what they want
- statements saying what is available within the organization, but including any notes about restrictions because of security, licences or other factors
- an analysis of the difference between these two sets of statements – a gap analysis (see the two articles by Singh)
- recommendations on providing further information services or on changes in information technology management that could assist information users
- the business cases used to justify access to information services.

Sharing these will help other information users (actual or potential) as well as demonstrate to the key decision makers in your user community that the information service means business.

Your intranet is a good channel for making news about information services available to everyone, and you can reinforce items there by e-mailing links to your key decision makers. If you are working in a non-corporate environment where there is no intranet, consider putting this information onto an internet website. It almost seems that these systems are being left behind in the stampede to Web 2.0 and 3.0, but senior users are more likely to read the intranet than a blog. (And if any organization succeeds in reducing its annual report to a meangingful 140-character Tweet, it will probably become world famous within 24 hours.)

Achieving cost benefits and making better use of budgets

Applying knowledge of user behaviour trends is a very important part of delivering the services that your users need, that are affordable, give value for money and are up to date. Clearly, best use of budgets will be made if resources are directed where they are needed and have the greatest effect.

We discussed earlier the need to explain why some spending decisions have been made, and that some modern services used in library and information services present problems to accounting systems. As a further example, financial managers can have problems dealing with the allocation of subscriptions expenditure under accruals accounting: money is laid out during one financial year for goods that will be delivered in instalments during the next financial year, and may not arrive when expected. As a result, unless the chief financial manager decides simply to treat subscription payments as a single transaction (regardless of the fact that the organization does not hold any asset in return for its initial outlay) the library financial officer will spend time moving sums of money around the budget sheet as each delivery arrives from the journals supplier.

But knowledge of the users' requirements can help improve the financial position: this knowledge can help the manager to decide:

- what mixture of print and electronic suits the organization best, allowing meaningful tendering and negotiation with suppliers
- whether or not to maintain physical collections and premises for any groups of users (clearly no academic institution is yet likely to make its library a 100% virtual presence, but this is happening frequently in public administration and business)
- whether collections need strengthening in any subject area; evidence of widespread informal information exchanges in the community's online spaces would suggest that adjustments are needed and that better value could be achieved from the budget
- what statistics from services such as Counter (www.projectcounter.org) or from survey instruments such as LibQual+(http://vamp.diglib.shrivenham.cranfield.ac.uk/perform ance/quality/libqual; Conyers, 2004) need further examination as evidence of the use or non-use being made of resources, and whether the library's impact is sufficient
- what level of confidence the library team can have in negotiations with suppliers – knowing to what extent information users are bypassing the library and using informal networks instead
- whether to remain with current consortia partners or to seek other partners (maybe other types of library) whose users appear to have more in common (Rowse, 2003).

Summary

All information services, large and small should ask questions about the role(s), function(s), effectiveness, costs, quality and delivery methods of existing services and systems. Such a review will need to be honest and perhaps at times brutal, and must strive to deliver improvements to users, to meet their needs. The results should be part of the strategic planning – both long and short term – that is essential in any organization. In the next chapter we look at how to keep track of changes in what your users want.

7

Keeping track of changes in what users want

In this chapter we look at:

➡ helping users to review their information needs
➡ how to keep track of changes in what users want
➡ how and where to find information about their changes
➡ surveys and statistics
➡ wider uses of information professional skills: reputation management
➡ know your users: building user loyalty and keeping it
➡ what next?

Helping users to review their information needs

At the end of the day it is the customer who really decides the quality of the services, by:

• making demands for improvements on an existing service
• asking for new services
• being willing to co-operate.

How do users express these demands and identify the need for new services? Here is the ideal opportunity to use information audit as a technique both to discover the information assets within the organization and to create a record of the ways in which your patrons are using them. It is also far more likely than when we originally developed our ideas of information audit that you will find information users who are quite content to be non-patrons of the LIS because they believe that the internet and other informal sources are accurately meeting all their requirements.

From your surveys of the users you will have knowledge of their information-seeking behaviour patterns. Under various headings we look at how to implement better strategic planning, the cost benefits and better use of budgets, better marketing and advertising, short and longer term gains and most of all at satisfied customers, wherever they are located and a very satisfied (but not complacent) management.

We cannot state too many times that the LIS manager and staff must ensure that the LIS should be central to the organization whatever the sector. If not, as we risk the dire consequences or cuts and decimation of services themselves. (This point is reinforced by Ford (2002) in the context of performance measurement.)

We noted a moment ago that users should expect to be willing to co-operate with the LIS. One way would clearly be to participate in surveys of requirements and use (and small incentives seem to work as well as anything more formal), but another means of co-operation is to observe licence terms and copyright. In the light of recent findings about the expectations of 'digital natives' and high profile cases of illegal file sharing, this point is worth emphasizing in information literacy work.

How to keep track of changes in what users want

Change is a given in any system. We have seen rapid changes in the LIS environment in recent years, such as those discussed in this chapter. An important support for the LIS is to have a methodology that can be adopted by others, e.g. the IT department, such as tracking user behaviour on websites and use of electronic services. The outputs from such a system provide agreed data in a common format that can be used by the LIS both for internal management purposes and to show upstream management how the service is operating. If the format is being used by other parts of the organization this will add validity. Some of the 'softer' observations (by which we mean for example output from horizon scanning rather than precise statistics of journal use) will be valuable in showing that the library's strategic plan takes account of current and likely future changes in user requirements.

Armed with this type of data, the LIS manager can put together the range of services that will meet the needs of the greatest number of users in the most cost-effective way. But remember that it can take considerable time from initial consultation and information audit to the final outcomes in the form of new or revised services. One of the classic examples is a consultation exercise carried out at the UK Royal College of Nursing that took a full two years to complete (Hyams, 2001).

How and where to find information about changes in service

How can information be gathered apart from using the standard reports from library management systems (which tend to report on things that are easy to count rather than things that are necessarily meaningful – that is, it is fairly simple to count 'one' when a publication is borrowed but that says nothing about whether it met the user's need at that time)?

External influences

Most organizations are affected to a greater or lesser degree by events in the outside world. The internet provides 24/7 access to news and comment, and it is now a simple matter (we would say not just simple but essential) to set up news alerts through Google and other search engines, and to subscribe to RSS feeds from your favoured websites. Services such as The Register (theregsiter.co.uk) and CNET (news.cnet.com) provide science and technology news that covers information management and political topics likely to affect you, or you could follow some of the increasing number of librarians who Twitter.

Professional activism

Being an involved library and information professional will pay additional dividends for your LIS. Membership of your national professional institute and its specialist groups will provide you with access to current information; being actively involved in the institute's work will increase your access to information through personal networks as well providing news and professional reading. Trade exhibitions, seminars, conferences and training courses are good places to hear about what other services have done for their users, and maybe to present your own experiences. Other professional bodies such as the Chartered Institute of Personnel and Development (CIPD) or the Chartered Management Institute (CMI) are worth monitoring for more general management news and publications.

Surveys and statistics

The LIS manager should survey managers or other representatives (depending on the type of community being served) to gather details of the types of information that members of that community need. This can be done using questionnaires and structured interviews; less controlled methods can be used such as sending feedback cards with library transactions but the results will probably be less reliable. The exercise should provide a clear understanding of the ways that users currently accesses information, and of the types of information that they use.

The results of information audits can (if the correct questions are used) identify specialist user needs together with details of the systems and services currently being used to meet those requirements. You will often find that people are using external sources such as their professional society or even the local public library because it does not occur to them to ask their own information specialists. It is worth retaining anonymized details of such discoveries as this kind of poor information-seeking behaviour carries considerable weight with upstream managers as evidence of the need to invest in library and information services.

Many electronic information services either contain or can provide statistical information about use of the service. Before the advent of 'all you can eat' charging for e-information, charges were based on statistics of connect time, hits and printout – but this of course gave no indication of the effectiveness of the expenditure, as ten minutes productive searching cost the same in connection time as leaving the terminal online while making a cup of coffee. If maximum value is to be obtained from 'always on' database subscriptions, statistics of use can also indicate other needs; for example a fall in use may indicate a requirement for training (or more training) in the use of the services available to users.

In recent years there has been a fairly rapid turnover in measures of performance and quality, and there is a mismatch between different sectors and even different geographic areas (for example, within the UK, the best value performance indicators for public libraries in England are no longer collected but a similar measure remains in force in Wales). In the academic sector there has been a plethora of projects aimed at improving the measurement of performance and systems: in the USA, the Association of Research Libraries (ARL; arl.org/stats) has produced some helpful material and sponsors the Library Assessment Conference (libraryassessment.org), which publishes its valuable presentations online and is associated with the MINES project (impact measurement, as distinct from total usage) – Project COUNTER, e-Metrics – or access (LibQUAL+®) (Plum et al., 2008); in the UK (in addition to COUNTER and LibQUAL+®) there are JUBILEE, EQUINOX and eVALUEd among others (Barton, 2004, covers the history but is now five years old).

Our point here is simply to note that although many projects have come and gone, and requirements to report to government likewise, some of these measures and systems may produce material that is valuable to you, and can help you make business cases in running your library or section. Do not throw out what works for you unless you are certain that its replacement is better or that you really don't have the time to continue running a system that tells you something worthwhile. Progress is not always linear and forward moving.

Wider uses of information professional skills: reputation management

We are aware of a number of new fields of work for information professionals, and believe these may help to influence people to decide whether to agree to a new or improved library or information centre. An example of one of these new fields is reputation management, which is a term that covers two ideas, both of which are typical librarian skills. One is ensuring that the quality and reputation of the services within the organization remains at the highest possible level, the other is looking after the good name of the organization and its services in the public arena. Branding and quality management are important elements of the first activity; the second extends into the area sometimes known as 'competitive intelligence' or even 'information warfare'. Recognition of the importance of this area has been slow in coming, although a recent article (Staines, 2009) makes the link to strategic planning in libraries, citing references that note the importance of the library's annual report in staking its budget claim and establishing its reputation.

The information centre manager will consider it important to provide a service to the user community of the highest possible standard, one that will support the organization in maintaining its reputation and where the flow of high quality information could be one of the things that the reputation is founded upon. But how does that translate into active management of the reputation of a service or organization?

The internet usability expert Jakob Nielsen is credited with the first widely accepted definition of this role: the reputation manager in his original definition was someone whose job was to co-ordinate large numbers of quality judgements provided by users of a service.

By 1999 Nielsen had refined his definition of reputation management as follows:

> an independent service that keeps track of the rated quality, credibility, or some other desirable metric for each element in a set. The things being rated will typically be websites, companies, products, or people, but in theory anything can have a reputation that users may want to look up before taking action or doing business. The reputation metrics are typically collected from other users who have had dealings with the thing that is being rated. Each user would indicate whether he or she was satisfied or dissatisfied. In the simplest case, the reputation of something is the average rating received from all users who have interacted with it in the past.
>
> (Nielsen, 1999)

Information professionals were involved at the beginning of the discipline of reputation management; their skills will help to maintain both their reputation within your organization and your organization's reputation in the market place. In some organizations this skill is necessarily taken further, and the LIS is involved in checking for mistruths and rumour concerning the organization, which are often started in order to destabilize a business rival, for example by affecting the share price. UK readers will be only too aware of this technique in the financial markets, for example in the 'shorting' of HBOS shares following the spread of rumours of financial instability in March 2009 – see http://news.bbc.co.uk/1/hi/business/7305039.stm.

But there is a further way of using the information professional's skills, which is to monitor your reputation, sharing what is found and ensuring that action is taken to remedy any untrue statements. This monitoring activity is very important in commercial circles but the technique can be applied to any sort of organization. You could just buy in press cuttings that mention your community or organization, but there is a wealth of information and comment on the internet that needs to be monitored, and new software has become available that allows you to build profiles and monitor positive and negative presentations of your reputation. The phenomenon of 'blogging' –

the writing of weblogs, which are like electronic diaries kept up to date on websites – has lent a new urgency to this area of work. Where employees can easily publish their thoughts (and your secrets!) to the whole world, and where both well-wishers and those who would do you harm have equal access to instant communication, this is an area that few can now ignore (Suitt, 2003)! To blogging should now be added Facebook, YouTube, Twitter, Flickr and the like.

We mentioned earlier in this chapter the need for users to co-operate and mentioned copyright compliance as an example. Blogging is another example: there should be a code of conduct in place – which was an issue in the fictitious case study used by Suitt – and it should be published. A few examples of good practice are available via the internet, such as that at IBM (ibm.com/blogs/zz/en/guidelines.html) (Cox, Martinez and Quinlan, 2008).

Copyright and intellectual property rights management are important issues in this context; and although this book is not about those topics, we note that a court case about copyright infringement or an admonishment by the Information Commissioner (in the UK – or CNIL in France, etc.) is not exactly going to be a glowing recommendation for your community's information management policies. Given that the Library is likely to have or share prime responsibility for these areas, we think that if there is no clear leader for this topic, the LIS should make itself that leader.

Users take account of both the organization's reputation and that of its information service in deciding, for example, whether to use information from the web without further corroboration, and services that collaborate with your information service take reputation partly into account when deciding the degree to which they will work in co-operation with you.

The area of reputation management continues to develop but provides a good example of the ways that information professional skill can be applied to a range of jobs. Think laterally and evaluate any areas that look as if they may be worthwhile investing time and money in.

Know your users: building user loyalty and keeping it

Having experience of building information services, electronic products and services over many years and keeping customers has given us an insight into the behaviour of customers. We observe that:

- they like to be consulted before, during and after the service or product is available
- they like customer care in all its aspects: emails, telephone calls, focus groups and so on
- they will tell others – see our comments above about managing the reputation of your service, and how it affects the overall reputation of your community
- they will let you know what the competition is doing, and how well
- they will tell you what is new that should be included if you are producing an electronic product
- they like to have contact with a staff member they know – think about the way account managers operate in public relations or personnel
- they do not like changes without consultation – so make sure that your communications are excellent!

What next?

The answer to this final question is simple: more of the same. Information needs and information resources both develop constantly, so what was a good match can become less good. Go to see your heaviest users at regular intervals and others as often as you can manage. Use the questionnaires as a basis to see what has altered and what has remained the same – and adjust your services accordingly!

Summary

It is essential to look closely at the organization's information needs and consult regularly with all the stakeholders if users are to become and remain satisfied. We have looked at a variety of tools such as information audit, communications and reputation management, as well as indicating where current practitioners see these issues going.

Our conclusions are many – based on working in various sectors during our professional lives, including running our own businesses, observing other successful organizations and most of all the desire to see all LIS flourish as the challenges in our information world continue to present themselves. We think these are huge but enjoyable challenges.

8

Tracking the future

In this chapter we look at some ways and methods of tracking the future, keeping ahead of the competition and anticipating your users' needs, by:

➡ keeping a watch on the wider changing world
➡ thinking about your networks – what can they tell you?
  — people
  — management networks
  — technical networks
➡ learning lessons
➡ changing customers' requirements
➡ making friends – what the suppliers are offering – both electronic and print sources
➡ making use of new ways of working and partnerships.

Keeping a watch on the wider changing world

It is essential to keep a very watchful eye on the wider changing world. What often develops in a different sector, e.g. retail, may be taken as the norm and expected in the information sector. As we have already seen, knowing your users and helping them to define their needs is one of the main ingredients that will achieve success in keeping at least one step ahead of their information demands. This is especially important when creating electronic information services, since the ready availability of e-services may mean that your users keep their requirements to themselves under the impression that they can get everything from the web or from desktop information services.

One of the other main ingredients for success is knowing what your users are planning – how they are going to demand products and services in future. These will have such an impact on the services that you are currently offering that your own customers may decide to take up the competitors' service. For example, if you are offering services to a specific group of users such as a research group and you wish to offer e-journals instead of paper-based services, you may find that the e-journal subscription agents decide to contact the research group directly. There is no real reason, if they receive a sufficiently cost-effective offer, why the research group should not take this offer up. They may feel that they would be in control of their own budget and of their choice of journals without having to deal with a third party – your information service.

Your networks – what can they tell you?

Your professional and personal networks will help you to create the most useful and relevant services to your users, and ensure that you remain as their first choice for information services.

What are your competitors offering in the way of services?

One way to find out is to ask them! After all, information professionals are a very gregarious bunch, and they will talk informally to others off the record. While you know that they would not divulge confidential information (and surely you would not ask them!) they will often share general information, and perhaps boast a little. You can often identify opportunities to adopt useful services in a way that helps your service without actually stealing anything.

What are competitors planning?

The considerations are similar to those above. However, it would be bad practice to rush to put other people's ideas into practice earlier than they manage to do so themselves.

What is happening in other information centres?

Here the entire world is at your disposal. For your own country, you can no doubt draw on the professional associations and the whole range of journals that provide news for the sector. Although a number of these will carry what are obviously news releases from software and library automation companies, you can see what services have been developed, and you may gain advantage from being an early adopter. For other countries, make sure that you read the various mailing lists (some of these are suggested in the appendices to this book) and look out for anything interesting. Even if the vendor does not operate in your country, you may be able to find the service from another provider, or if the possibility is tempting enough, the vendor may even look for a local agent.

What are information services in other sectors offering?

Don't confine your researches to your own sector alone. There may be some ideas in other areas of information work that you can adapt for your own information centre. In some sectors there is considerable investment and new services are often created. That is especially true in the present climate of mergers and rebranding, so – although not everyone is happy about some of the changes – there may be new offers that might be more appropriate to your own areas of work, and to what your customers are doing.

Many organizations have a range of information needs that are not always directly connected to their core business, and providing information services to people with less common requirements is often disproportionately expensive. So it may be that you can afford to buy into a new service from a supplier who has repackaged that information either by adding information that you do require, or by coming up with a new price package that suits you better.

People

People related to your service can be classified in a number of ways. In one way of looking at it, you will have users who are frequent, irregular or non-users, or those who are information literate or those who need training. You will number suppliers among your contacts, and some of them may be internal suppliers, for example if they contribute to a database. You need to come up with a strategy to keep in touch with all of these people.

Are their information needs changing? Do they have plans for different types of work where new services may be important? What are their future plans and how does your service need to adapt to meet their needs?

During your education, training and your various jobs you will have come into contact with a wide range of people from different disciplines and walks of life. Many of them will keep in touch even though they are now working in other countries or organizations. They form an invisible network, an invisible college, of people who can give you advice or tell you about the latest developments where they are. Many people now have some kind of take on information services, as a user if not as a provider, and their ideas can often help you. Anyway, many of them will be only too pleased to hear from you!

Mentors and gurus

Mentoring can be a formal or informal arrangement that can be of benefit to information specialists. Among the benefits is the possibility to sound out new ideas and thoughts, and expand on them before using them in one's own organization.

In our professional careers we have both had welcome opportunities to present ideas to people at senior levels in the profession and in the organization. They have been able to help to develop plans, and assure us that an idea is workable. However, the more senior the position that you reach, the less likely you are to be able to discuss ideas about information services with your peers within the organization. In many cases other senior people have little idea or interest about these areas of work.

There are two points that emerge. One is that you may need to re-develop the relationships that you have with others who now hold senior positions in other organizations as they will better understand the issues that now concern you. In the context of developing e-services, for example, they are very likely to be dealing with issues around electronic service delivery, and the huge cultural changes that this requires in many organizations. The other point is that you may need to identify new mentors who can help with your current concerns. Although you will almost certainly want to keep in touch with those who have helped you through the earlier stages of your career, you may well find that, with the best will in the world, they no longer have the understanding that you require of the new issues that you face.

Management networks

What is the understanding of senior people of the problems that you need to tackle? Can a different network, probably with nothing to do with information management, help you better? (This is possibly the equivalent of 'should I get out more?', but taking a broad view of the available networks may well suggest that you could profitably meet that old friend who talked of another group where the members had similar backgrounds to your own senior managers. What could these people offer you once they know of your professional interest in electronic services?)

So, we have noted that for a strategic approach to information services in an organization, you will need to manage an approach to the most senior levels. You are likely to need to show them what is possible in order to get their involvement and support for the information service on the financial and communications fronts.

Especially for electronic services, the financial aspects are likely to be more difficult than the public relations angles. The business case for electronic services is not obvious, and you will need to produce a convincing argument in favour of it.

Regular meetings are likely to be a valuable tool, which can help to place plans of work for new services into a business context, and equally ensure that plans for the organization take account of the information services' ability to provide appropriate services. All too often parts of an organization are the target of direct sales pitches that end up on the desks of senior management as firm proposals for new business activity involving the unnecessary duplication of electronic information services. Why take out new subscriptions to electronic services when those used by the information service have spare capacity at no additional cost? Why use untrained people to search when there is a professional service that can keep down the costs to the organization as a whole and perhaps broker the take-up of unused time on a subscription service in order to manage costs overall?

Technical networks

Does your information service manage your organization's computer services department? If not, you will need to ensure that the technical team understands the information services' technical requirements.

We have heard of organizations where the technical services never fully understood what the information team needed – despite, in one example we found, taking people to the USA to show them exactly what was needed, how it had been implemented and the steps that had been taken to set up the necessary network. This took place, of course, in the early days of technological developments for information services. A memorable phrase used by one of the technical people was, 'Yes, it is all technically possible, but we can't do it.' Of course life has become much easier with more reliable software and more robust networks.

An excellent way to achieve good working relations is to use a service level agreement (SLA) as the basis of meetings with the computer services manager and staff. The formal agenda should include work fulfilled in the time between meetings, and performance against the requirements of the SLA. The SLA should be drawn up in conjunction with the computer services department, ensuring a good understanding of responsibilities.

Why a service level agreement is important

In an SLA, it is essential that all levels of staff are involved in the compilation of the agreement. This is because everyone's personal performance, their understanding of the levels of services to be achieved and the timescales within which these levels of services are to be given are all contained in the agreement. Job descriptions and the required levels of performance will be derived from the SLA through the business planning process. The job appraisal exercise a year later is not the time to discover that there are problems. So, you need to be aware of the full implications of an SLA at whatever level you are working.

It is often the person working at the enquiry desk, in the interlibrary loans or search service section, or in the ordering section who has the most detailed knowledge of the systems that will have to meet any agreements. For instance, it is no good agreeing to demands from the technical services department to take down the computer system at a certain time of the day when you and your staff know that this is the peak time for providing services for the users.

Features of a service level agreement

Service level agreements were first widely used to manage relations with corporate computing sections and have a number of features that reflect their origins. They are often a feature of quality management systems where their precision aids the process of definition of products and services. They clarify the relationship between the supplier and the customer by setting out expectations and responsibilities, and the commitment of both parties to the agreement. Setting out the customer's responsibilities in the contract as well as the supplier's should avoid any arguments that can arise unnecessarily, for example where the customer has more details about a requested document than they actually reveal. Most information workers will have experienced the situation where a customer asks vaguely for some reference only to find that they have all the details in front of them but omitted to tell the information section! The implied suggestion is that it is up to the supplier to find the item required with no further clues. And the SLA is a planning tool for the supplier, by allowing prediction of troughs and peaks of activity.

The SLA is prescriptive, but it should say what is to be done rather than how. To describe and define the required result is useful: to say how things are to be done is unnecessarily restrictive. The supplier should be free to achieve the required result in the best way possible without having to adapt that solution to some local routine that would better be changed to some more efficient way of working.

If a standard service is provided then the agreement need only refer to the standard terms and then list the variations, exceptions or enhancements. This can be particularly useful in the case of electronic services, since many of them are described in standard brochures. The combination of these service descriptions with statements of technical requirements and any variations or exceptions that have been agreed may be all that is needed.

We believe that having a SLA will help everyone involved. The SLA will help people understand issues such as what services are needed, the deadlines to be met, and the necessary steps that should be undertaken when services such as computer services fail. An SLA provides the opportunity to revise the agreements as developments take place, for example when new services become available which are of interest to users of the LIS. The second edition of our book *The Complete Guide to Preparing and Implementing Service Level Agreements* (Pantry and Griffiths, 2nd edn, 2001) shows in detail how to set up such agreements and equally importantly how to keep the SLA revised.

Winning others across

Because so many people will be involved in creating information services, you will need to win others across at all stages of the creation and maintenance of the service. Get the organization's senior management approval to the strategic concept before going out to talk to a range of people in the organization.

Among those you need to contact are:

- the information services staff who will be helping you to implement the service – what are their concerns about electronic services and their role in providing them?
- the other service providers in the organization – what impact do your plans have on them (for example by undercutting an existing service, or by placing additional load on networks)?
- service providers outside the organization, such as journal suppliers who may need to support the licensing of electronic data, or negotiate new terms – if you do not win these suppliers across, you may find yourself looking at a delay while you re-tender contracts through the European official journal
- various user groups – your customers may well have an opinion on the services you want to introduce. You may even have to balance the requirements of several groups, e.g. in an academic situation, students and the lecturing staff, or in a business environment the business managers and researchers.

You should also open discussions with known non-users, particularly those in senior positions. Your proposed services may well be of benefit to them, and to less frequent users of the service. You could well attract them with a modern way of delivering information to their workstations.

Whichever is your starting point you will need to have discussions, and formal and informal meetings, to take people along so that they feel that they have ownership in the creation of the new service. Ask for the opinions of all levels of staff at the outset, so that you do not ignore the needs of managers or of front-line workers, or base your proposals on second-hand accounts of their requirements.

Staff often have ideas about service management or can describe good practice that they have seen working elsewhere, and allow them to expand their roles and careers. They will buy in more readily if they have a feeling of involvement in the decisions. Explaining the strategy to people as early as possible will provide the opportunity to delegate parts of the work. Small groups of staff with particular knowledge or interest will be able to develop in particular subject fields or deal with particular suppliers. They will know how to bring in new ideas; and by ensuring that there is a forum where staff can exchange news with other members of the other working groups, you can ensure that everyone keeps in touch with this work.

A final word – do ensure that staff representatives are kept fully informed. It's important that they feel comfortable with the proposals, and that you know they understand the potential opportunities as well as dealing with any fears they may have about future job security or changes.

Users

The users themselves are perhaps the most difficult groups when it comes to winning their confidence. Many people do not like change, are suspicious of services that do away with the 'comfort blanket' of paper-based services. If you are making radical changes keep informing the users about:

- what is planned
- how the changes will be managed
- how the changes will affect them
- what, if any, training will be needed
- for whom training will be provided, and how long it will take.

No doubt, if the costs are allocated to their department users will insist on knowing the details of any increases. You will need to have your arguments ready to answer questions and deal with any possible dissent. You will be able to describe your customers' current information needs and you will be able to demonstrate the cost benefits of information services. Bringing your customers into your confidence at an early stage will strengthen their commitment to you. It should ensure that they refer on to you when suppliers and other information services approach them directly and offer services. You could also point out that your understanding of electronic services will probably save them money. Not only will you know how to provide the services within any package at the best value prices by selecting them from the best value source, but you will be able to ensure that competitors have not cut prices by leaving out any essential but expensive elements!

Keep in touch with your users' current and future needs. They will be increasingly dependent on good quality information in the future, and will probably be overwhelmed by the sheer volume if they go looking for it themselves on the world wide web!

Publishing

The models of journal and book publishing and distribution are in a period of rapid change. The number of suppliers and journal consolidators has reduced in recent years but those that remain are having to work hard for their income. Keep an eye on the commercial publishing world to find out what they are offering, and how they deliver to their customers. Special interest groups such as the UK Serials Group bring together suppliers (see next section) and consumers, and their conferences and journals contain useful updates and indications of future trends in publication and delivery.

Suppliers

Your suppliers are a key ally in keeping you up to date with new developments that will keep you one step ahead of your users. Regular contact between your information service and suppliers will provide you with news of what is changing and what is being developed to improve the experience of LIS patrons. Suppliers are usually keen to maintain regular contact; if you have outsourced selection or taken journal consolidation services you will almost certainly have regular review meetings (if not, why not?) where new developments can be discussed and newly identified needs of your users proposed to your supplier for consideration.

Suppliers on the web

In recent years the internet has provided a growingly important platform for the development of electronic information services. Suppliers and publishers routinely put information onto the internet as a viable means of document supply.

Web-based delivery allows suppliers to offer an enhanced range of services rather than simply providing administrative support such as announcement of publication dates and delays. Full text and bibliographic databases that are constantly updated are available from various sources.

Electronic journals

In the last ten years there has been a huge growth in the range and number of electronic journals available for use by information services and other subscribers. We have seen the growth of integrated services and portals such as the Emerald Library, delivering a wide range of journals and allowing users to navigate to and download articles in formats such as Portable Document Format (.pdf). The agent or publisher thus takes care of much of the day-to-day administration, including handling of permissions and access control.

Services such as this can lead end users to behave like children let loose in a sweetshop. The sheer quantity of information available can lead them to gorge on uncontrolled amounts of articles and other electronic resources. Information professionals can apply their skills to this mass of information and analyse new materials in order to highlight the most relevant items, which they can suggest to users. The information service thus remains in control of the process, and is ready for any follow-up demands (for example, for copies of articles referred to in the electronic documents). Contents listings can be scrutinized in a similar way, perhaps ensuring that copies of articles in themed issues can quickly be sourced, or that articles by key authors in particular subject fields are added to reference bibliographies. Depending on licensing agreements, copies of key items can be downloaded and added to shared folders.

Using integrated services to head off customer requests

You can make use of vendors' integrated services to head off anticipated user requests. The information centre's life will be easier if you are able to handle the volume of demand for particular items or journals, and e-journals can provide the means to do so. An example case study is discussed below.

A medium sized library circulates journals but some key titles can take up to two years to circulate since they go to a long list of people and tend to contain a number of important articles. Many users low down the circulation never see the journal at all, or if it reaches them too many articles are out of date. Nobody knows who has got a particular issue when it is needed in a hurry. The information centre finds itself sending off for British Library Document Supply Services article copies, or buying extra copies of important journal issues. The solution arrived at in this case might involve keeping the journals in the library, then circulating contents lists containing hyperlinks to an online full text service. This could show reduced costs overall, and ensure that important journals remain available in the information centre. (Since your licence probably demands that you subscribe to the paper version to get electronic access, why not put the paper copies somewhere they can be useful? An unexpected bonus could be greater use of the information centre.)

The administration facilities provided by e-journal suppliers can also help to inform customers without the need for your staff to spend time on dealing with routine enquiries such as the expected arrival date of the next issue of a journal. Suppliers will typically issue bulletins of such information that can be published on an intranet, while some library management systems will allow users to view check-in screens for predicted dates. Other information relating to licensing or costs can also be included on your intranet.

Dealing with particular users in organizations

In this and other publications we have discussed the different needs of the various user groups in your organization. Our view is that meeting these requirements can be as much an issue of management or of communications as of having particular library and information professional skills.

Senior managers may be intrigued by the opportunities you are developing using e-services, but be ignorant of some of the constraints that you face. Why cannot these electronic journals be rolled out to the whole organization, regardless of licences? Why cannot the subscription to paper be cancelled now you have all this information? Why does the information centre need so much space in this case?

Information technology managers may be concerned by the level of demand being placed on their networks, and insist that your services are slowing down access to computing facilities generally, or the performance of the intranet.

Research areas may demand that their most heavily used journals are placed on the network even where costs, licences or technical compatibility may be issues. And so on.

None of these is a show-stopping problem. But they are examples of problems that can be anticipated, like others that will spring to mind in the context of your own organization. You can be ready with financial information such as the details of the increased costs that would be incurred by purchasing further simultaneous user licences. You can obtain some reliable predictions of the additional network load imposed by a particular supplier's service from that supplier. You can discover from agents what technical standards need to be met in order to run a particular product or – for example – to be able to read a particular journal at a Mac rather than a Windows PC.

The same skills and contacts that you use to keep ahead of the customer when dealing with new information services can be used here. The same communications skills that you use when issuing information about the library to users can help you to reinforce the message that your service is on top of all these questions, and thinks ahead.

In order to manage demand within available resources you need to anticipate user needs. By offering information and services based on the use of electronic delivery that will meet these requirements, you can gain in several ways:

- Customer requirements are met rapidly by services already tuned to their needs.
- Demand on the information centre is managed within resources; in particular, time pressures are reduced by improved availability of the most requested information.
- Costs can be managed more readily.
- The profile of the information centre as a source of timely, relevant information and its reputation for being in touch with developments in information supply are both enhanced.

To achieve this you will need to involve a range of players, including those we have considered here.

Perhaps the most difficult job an information provider has to do is to get clear understanding of the organization so as to be able to provide an information service which is *central* to the organization.

External sources of information

You will find that individuals may use external sources to obtain information without going through the library or information centre. It may be that they are using their professional organization to obtain information. If your organization pays for their membership it may be possible to make an arrangement whereby you can have access also to this external source.

Other external sources which you will need to define is attendance by staff members at conferences and seminars, where they obtain information that may be of further use to the organization. Arrangements could be made to obtain this information for indexing purposes allowing the individual to keep on extended loan the documents. This way others in the organization can share the new knowledge.

So where are the customers?

In any organization whether it is large or small there are always people who perhaps have a fair idea of what information they need for their jobs. However, there are many who do not think they need any information ever! There is a range of customers and potential customers in all organizations. Some may need to be shown that information is vital for their work and perhaps their long term promotion.

These customers may fall into the following categories:

- those who never use information
- those who are timid but would like to know more about information
- sporadic users – think they have all the information they need but may condescend to use the information service from time to time
- devoted information users who make good use of all the services on offer.

New types of library behaviour

The widespread adoption of social media and their associated technologies have led to a rapid change in user behaviour. Social networking offers new forms of library use such as 'chat reference' using instant messaging services (either computer system based or mobile telephone based), and users increasingly see no reason why they should expect a different level of type of service when using the LIS. It becomes seen as a shortcoming of the service if it cannot offer the type of facility offered by other providers.

Charles Martell (2008) in his article 'The absent user' notes that the use of the physical collections and services of academic libraries continues to plummet, with some exceptions, while use of electronic networked resources skyrockets. This article frames the extent of this decline with a focus on circulation and reference usage among the American Research Libraries (ARL) University, Medical and Law Libraries, the Ivy League, other associations, systems, and individual libraries.

In 'Connecting 24/5 to millennials', Anne Cooper Moore and Kimberly A. Wells (2009) investigate user preferences for reference and technical support, services and facilities featured in an academic library and Learning Commons through a 23-item questionnaire distributed to building entrants during one 24-hour period on 14 March, 2006. Results revealed a strong preference for face-to-face assistance (including roving), suggested enhancements and documented user demographics.

Where do people go for their information if not to the information service?

There are a number of reasons why people do not use their information services. Many people may lack personal information-searching skills themselves and are unaware of the wealth of information which can be obtained through the information service. Likewise many people think they know the answers to all their information needs and carry on without checking to see if other newer, more up-to-date information exists.

When discussing their information needs you need to press home to users the crucial question 'On what information do you depend to do your job?'

When is the information needed?

It is essential to find out from the information user how quickly the information they are seeking is really needed. You will need to define the timescales so that everyone is working from the same starting point. Perhaps a list of definitions will help to achieve consistency and also verify in the customer's mind by which time the information is really required:

> *desperate* – must have the information within the hour if possible (you may have to remind the customer that extra payment is needed for this kind of speedy service, especially if this falls within your service level agreement)
> *urgent* – needed within 24 hours
> *as soon as possible* – needed within five working days
> *need* – would like at some point in the next two weeks.

How is the information required to be presented?

It is essential when a customer seeks information to ask how the presentation of the information should be made. It may be required by e-mail; or it may be necessary to summarize it and follow it with other data. The references may be required to be organized by author or chronologically arranged. Does your service offer Endnotes or other similiar service? In *Success at the Enquiry Desk* (2006), Tim Owen stresses the importance of presenting the information in a professional manner. Do check with the information seeker that the services are required or you will be wasting your time and theirs plus valuable resources!

User expectations

Even ten years ago it was becoming apparent that the expectations of LIS users were growing, and that as a result they had become more demanding, as this extract from an article in *New Library World* demonstrates:

Users are described as customers in many environments, ranging from local government to higher education. In some contexts financial transactions take place, such as the payment of university fees, which give rise not only to expectations of a level of service but to a feeling that the service is open to criticism (and perhaps financial redress) if it does not meet those expectations.

It is critical that users do perceive quality in our service delivery as certain events have served to heighten their perception of themselves as paying customers. From September 1998, students in higher education establishments in England and Wales began paying a contribution of up to £1,000 per annum towards their tuition fees. A proportion of this should go to the library to help pay for services. As a result of this development, our users will perceive themselves more directly to be our customers, in that they are paying for their education directly, as opposed to indirectly, through taxes. Thus, the exchange relationship becomes closer to the classic model delineated in traditional goods marketing.

(Broady-Preston and Preston, 1999)

Technological change

The networked campus together with the presence of legitimate users of the LIS located beyond the campus have eliminated the need for many users to be physically present in the library. Although this offers opportunities to extend electronic services and make them available to a wide range of current and new users, this change also removes the interaction between library staff and users. The research to date suggests that user behaviour changes, for example because the library staff become anonymous to the users; therefore there is no bond or loyalty between user and library, and contact is provided by a machine interface. This change tends to emphasize the widely observed phenomenon of users believing that all information is available (for free) on the internet without the need for any intervention by professional or trained library staff, and that students and other users therefore do not need to visit or even use their library, and it becomes even more necessary for LIS professionals to advocate the continuing need for the service and its professional staff.

Social and personal change

The most recent development of the technological issue is the very rapid development of personalized and socialized technology. Especially among student users, library patrons are not only familiar with social technology (services such as Facebook, MySpace and Twitter – a range of services that is growing almost daily) and mobile applications, but these are an integral part of their lives. Many of these services feature personalized applications, and users are observed to look for the potential to personalize library services just as any other similar application delivered through computer networks.

Meeting the user's new expectations

Library and information services have evolved greatly in the past and will continue to do so; what is exceptional is not so much the change as the rate of change now taking place. In the early 21st century UK an additional complication is that in a number of sectors, notably but not only in public libraries, the service is defined not so much by the user's expectations but by an often politically driven statement of the user's expectations.

This creates various layers of difficulty in assessing user requirements. The first is that the users themselves may have outdated views of libraries, so that they express requirements in terms of what they think should be available rather than what they want and could make use of. Internet access, for example, has come about as much because of the People's Network programme as because users have demanded it from their library services. People have a view of libraries, reinforced by media stereotypes, so they are surprised by modern libraries:

Gosport Discovery Centre
> This is a lovely place to come and relax, it is not a normal library
> where you have to be quiet. Children are very welcome with a
> great selection of kids books –
> Posted by morganmoo to qype.co.uk, which collects and rates
> user reviews of entertainment venues, 21 September 2008
> www.qype.co.uk/place/207829-Gosport-Discovery-Centre-and-
> Gosport-Gallery-Gosport

Keeping up with expectations – some unconventional ideas

How can you keep in touch with user expectations and requirements, and decide which you will satisfy as part of your business planning? We talked earlier (in Chapter 5) about more conventional methods like user surveys, but there are other resources that will fill in the gaps and that can be used to provide more instant and continual feedback that will tell you how things are going.

Let's think back to the findings of the 'Google Generation' report: users (all users, the report argues, rather than 'digital natives' alone) multitask rather than carrying out a single task (such as reading a single report); users prefer quick information in the form of easily digested chunks rather than full text; and they 'power browse' looking for relevant information. Marydee Ojala in an editorial to an issue of *Online* in 2006 set out the issue as follows:

> Today's library users are more likely to use their personal computers to access information than to walk down a library aisle. They're . . . ready to swoop and pluck the juiciest morsel they see. Scholars are often exasperated by these behaviors of information end users. They want books read cover to cover. They prefer methodological rigor. They want publications to be viewed as complete entities, not as bits and pieces pulled out to support whatever paper a student is writing or point of view a researcher is espousing. Today's end users . . . are not methodical. They do not read books from cover to cover, unless it's fiction with a strong

plot that requires starting at the first page and ending on the last. They multitask. They instant message while searching the Internet, listening to music, and blogging. I believe, however, that this is the natural outgrowth of the free-text searching on full-text documents that developed in the early to mid-1980s. It's the next level of online. We are moving from an information environment dominated by publication entities to one of snippets and pieces . . . The methodology changes from one that starts at the upper left of a page . . . and continues line by line, row by row, to the lower right, to one that celebrates peripheral vision, the gathering of bits and pieces to make a whole, and data overlays.

(Ojala, 2006)

These new behaviours mean that you need to think differently in creating your response and keeping your LIS at the forefront. What are your users saying that they need, or that they are having difficulty in finding? Where are they saying it, bearing in mind that they are unlikely to wait for your next user survey to express opinions!

Summary

The final results of the analysis of your user survey should give you a unique understanding not only of the organization, but of the behaviour of the information users in your organization. You should also be aware who uses information to the fullest extent, who needs information, the shortcomings of the telecommunications, computer and other services. Most of all you will really know the customers in your organization. So good luck with the further information services you will need to create to satisfy the information needs of the organization and its users and the promotion and marketing activities you will need to undertake.

9

Future perfect?

In this final chapter we look at what could really make a difference in the future:

➡ some recommendations
➡ a possible patron?
➡ politics
➡ the library as place
➡ shh, this is a digital library
➡ shaping a modern library
➡ challenges for the future.

Throughout the book we have identified many actions that can be done to give your users the LIS they want. There are challenges and opportunities that can be taken up to rethink creatively and take the initiative in getting the users to articulate what they need, keep the dialogue open with them and set the pace. You have access to all the information you need to keep ahead of the game if you want!

Some recommendations

When the contributors in *Digital Consumers* (Nicholas and Rowlands, 2008) were asked to each provide one suggestion as what should be a priority when offering services to users they came up with the following in order of priority:

1 Live with the prospect of constant change.
2 Establish a link with information provisions and access/outcomes.
3 Keep it simple.
4 Do not be seduced by digital fashions, they will all disappear.
5 Get social.
6 Hold on to physical space.

Information people will be pleased to know that no one said 'the last one out turn the lights off', although a few were close to saying this.

A number of recommendations for libraries are suggested by Thomas Frey of The DaVinci Institute who says of the future (Frey, 2006): 'libraries are in a unique position. Since most people have fond memories of their times growing up in libraries, and there are no real "library hater" organizations, most libraries have the luxury of time to reinvent themselves.' He agrees with us that the role of a library within a community is changing and most of all the way people are interacting with the LIS and the services offered are also changing. The best advice is to enjoy the journey and relish in the wonderment of what tomorrow may bring and continue to accept the challenges and changes.

The following recommendations should allow libraries and their managers to arrive at their own best solutions:

1 Evaluate the library *experience*. Begin the process of testing patrons' opinions, ideas and thoughts, and figure out how to get at the heart of the things that matter most in your community. Survey both the community at large and the people who walk through the library doors.
2 Embrace *new information technologies*. New tech products are being introduced daily and the vast majority of people are totally lost when it comes to deciding what to use and what to stay away from. Since no organization has stepped up to take the lead in helping the general public understand the new technology, this is a perfect opportunity for libraries. Libraries need to become a resource for as well as being the experts in each of the new

technologies. Some ways that this could be done are to:

a create a technology advisory board and stay in close communication with them

b recruit tech savvy members of the community to hold monthly discussion panels where the community at large is invited to join in the discussions

c develop a guest lecture series on the new technologies.

3 *Preserve the memories of your own communities.* Although most libraries have become the document archive of their community, the memories of a community span much more than just documents. What did it sound like to drive down the High Street in 1950? What did it smell like to walk into Joe's Bakery in the early mornings of 1965? Who are the people in these community photos and why were they important? Memories come in many shapes and forms. Don't let yours disappear.

4 *Experiment with creative spaces so the future role of the library can define itself.* Since the role of the library 20 years from now is still a mystery, we recommend that libraries put together creative spaces so staff members, library users, and the community at large can experiment and determine what ideas are drawing attention and getting traction. Some possible uses for these creative spaces include:

a band practice rooms

b podcasting stations

c blogger stations

d art studios

e recording studios

f video studios

g imagination rooms

h theatre-drama practice rooms

Is there a patron?

Given that the ultimate aim must be *to please all the people/users all of the time* your professional life is always going to be an uphill struggle without support and endorsement within your community or organization. Therefore if you have the support of management, or better still a management champion or patron, your service will have a distinct advantage.

Is the age of the patron dead? We say not, so what might this management patronage consist of? First of all, we should identify who could provide it, so that we can see what kind of support could be forthcoming. In a business or an existing public sector body the management role is pretty clear – it's a person who is more senior than the information service manager and to whom that manager reports. In a community it's a senior person who has influence or some other kind of central position, such as a head teacher or deputy, or perhaps someone who sits on the board of a learned society or professional college. Whoever it is, the characteristics of that person will include their position of influence or authority, and usually their seniority to the information service manager. It makes some difference whether they are directly responsible for managing the information service manager, since that will affect their ability to instruct the manager to carry out particular tasks or offer particular services, or merely pass back suggestions and comments from others.

Being the information service manager's direct boss will also affect the degree of shared interest that the person will have in the success of the information centre so far as their own performance goes.

We hope that support from your manager (whoever it is) is interested rather than dutiful, and reflects a genuine wish to be responsible for your service rather than a kind of 'Oh dear, I've been given the library' kind of attitude. We know of one information service that is currently really struggling to survive and the manager in charge keeps saying 'prove to me why the users want the service'. When the users – including members of the public – give the reasons they want the service, such as it is 'a unique collection in the UK', that manager is only interested in the bottom line – money! The manager just does not understand and worse still does not listen.

But a manager should be pleased to be responsible for the people, the service and place that provide so many members of any organization or community with one of their consistently positive experiences. Keep copies of the compliments that the service receives, and report on them at regular intervals, for example in your monthly or other regular report to management. Even if there is a reporting template, such bouquets can be listed or extracted in an annex to the main monthly report.

Many surveys show how well the users of library and information services regard the services they receive and the people who provide them. You should take advantage of this goodwill by surveying your users (even if they already send you unsolicited testimonials!) and by presenting the results to your management. Managers will soon realize what a treasure they are responsible for. Remind them to tell others about the facilities and services that you offer and keep them aware of your achievements. Emphasize too how the information service can provide invaluable support to the projects that may be taking place within the organization, or the activities of the community. You should consider how you can let your patron share some of the kudos of the LIS, perhaps by acknowledging the senior level support you get when making reports or presentation.

Non-specialist managers are notoriously unaware of what library and information services do, and need to be shown. We hope that you get regular time with whoever manages your particular community – if not, ask whether you can meet regularly and keep them up to date with what is going on. Pitch what you say to their needs, not exclusively your own. Think how your service fits into their agenda, so that you can give them news and information that they can use in turn when somebody more senior asks: 'What goes on in that library or information centre?' The exact message will obviously vary depending on the type of organization or community where you provide your service; in special libraries you will probably have to spend more time showing the value your service adds than (for example) in an academic library, where there is a broad acceptance that any credible institution must be supported by high quality LIS capable of being measured by nationally accepted standards. While an immediate response by managers in a nonacademic environment might be 'This is not an academic institution so does not need that quality of LIS', it could be worth asking 'Would you consider contracting with academia to carry out research or other work on our behalf?' If the answer is yes then it could be worth looking again at the assumption that providing a high quality LIS is only a valid choice for the largest organizations.

We think that managers have responsibility to their teams just as the team members have responsibilities to their managers. Managers with top level responsibility for LIS should:

- take the time to understand what it is you and your team do
- understand why you must be the ones to do it (this means teaching your patrons the truth about the Internet and what is not on it)
- provide regular feedback on what the organization or community is doing so that you can tailor services to the needs that those activities create
- provide support up and down the line that comes from an informed interest (beware the manager who says, 'X says this about you, how do I respond to that?' – if that happens, book a one-to-one awareness session to enlighten them as soon as possible!)
- give a commitment to take your good news stories to the wider audience of movers and shakers in your community.

What is your side of the deal in return? It is to be professional at all times: and as part of that professionalism you must do your best for your patron as well as your community.

Can your patron help you with financial issues? Whether you work for a public body or a private one, there will be some kind of financial structure within which you must work. If you are in a fee-collecting organization of some sort, you may even be faced with a situation where you must price your services in order to cover salaries, cost of materials and perhaps the cost of accommodation, light, heat and so on. Most organizations do this by working out what money they have and what they will spend over a period of one financial year (which may be the calendar year or some other 12-month period such as April to March to coincide with the fiscal or tax year). If the situation is reasonably straightforward, you will receive a sum of money each year that is supposed to provide for your expected costs. You are almost certain to have to account for this, and even if this function is carried out centrally you would be well advised to keep some sort of record (which might be in your library housekeeping system) to tell you how much you have spent, because bills are not always paid straight away by finance departments, so you could appear to have more funds remaining than is actually the case.

Two issues need to be dealt with in terms of management involvement and patronage. One is the question of rising subscription costs; the other is making sure that someone in a position of influence understands the nature of subscription management.

Rising subscription costs have been a talking point for many years. Publishers have argued the need to maintain profitability in order to publish research findings, and librarians have pointed to diminishing funds, which result in their need to cut purchases. As we have seen in other parts of this book, deals have been brokered and new models of service delivery, such as the information commons, have been developed in response. Your supporters need to understand this equation, and that while publishers need to make a business of publishing there are ways to deal with rising costs: you should emphasize that wholesale cuts are not the only one.

The other financial issue is often bewilderment in the accounting section that although the LIS was allocated a large sum of money for the expensive subscriptions that it argued for, halfway through the financial year almost none of the money has been spent! LIS professionals will recognize the very seasonal manner in which expenditure occurs, and that annual subscriptions are paid on a single invoice (or a few at most) even if some forms of accounting then require costs to be moved around a monthly accounts system to show the expenditure on the summer issue of a journal to be posted in June rather than the previous December. (This assumes that subscriptions can be reclaimed if cancelled, which is not always the case.)

Patrons deserve to know what they are sponsoring, including the more uncommon features of the financial cycle. Your sponsors should be getting the LIS they want, which is one that does not spring nasty surprises in its accounts!

Politics

It's hard to manage a modern LIS without taking politics into account. Perhaps the effects are felt less in special libraries, although even in this sector some services (such as government department libraries) are affected by political change and can find themselves being merged or transferred, or subjected to new financial regimes.

In the public library sector, debate has grown over what is meant by a 'comprehensive and efficient' library service, which is spoken of in the Public Libraries and Museums Act 1964 as a requirement for all local authorities, but there is no definition of what this actually is.

The MLA (Museums, Libraries and Archives Council) proposed that the following elements should exist as part of a library service (MLA, 2009):

- access (free of charge) for the public of all ages and regardless of income, within a reasonable travelling distance
- a range of services, not only (and obviously) books, but also internet access (free, ideally), information of all kinds (coupled with expertise and advice), reader groups (for various ages and needs) and community space in which to read and learn
- a range of learning programmes and skills development to meet skills needs; not just internet access but programmes designed to meet increasing demand from users affected by the economic downturn
- integration, where possible and appropriate, with one or more of the other community services provided for local people, for instance with PCT surgeries, FE colleges, museums, learning

centres and children's centres
- opening hours that meet the communities' needs, based on thorough consultation and full engagement with a wide range of users and user-groups
- awareness of other facilities in each specific locality (or lack of them), to enable an appreciation of the rounded nature of the service offered by individual libraries.

The MLA argued further for the need to assess alternatives where library closures are needed as part of development plans, and to emphasize the contribution of the service to the community. This political aspect of LIS provision draws attention to the role of the library and information centre in its community, and to the issues around any service that relate to its physical place in a geographic location (whether that is a town or business premises of some kind), and the way that the users come – or don't physically come – to the place that the library occupies.

The library as place

In the last ten years libraries in the academic sector have been affected by rapid and significant changes in learning styles; these have caused radical alterations in library user needs and consequently the way that those users assess their libraries. These changes include a transition over a short period of time from print to virtual sources and the consequent freeing of users from the physical confines of the library and the places that it stores its collections. Other sectors, particularly special and corporate information services, have also been affected by similar changes, for example because of pressure to reduce use of physical space in expensive inner-city offices.

All of these changes have created a new focus on the library as a physical space, and on how this space is perceived and used by LIS customers. This focus has been emphasized by the inclusion of 'library as place' in one set of widely used performance indicators, as we shall see in a moment.

There is a danger of regarding current uses of LIS space as sacrosanct and therefore of refusing to consider changing the use of library space (for example to provide coffee lounges and 'noisy' spaces, which are seen to go against the 'traditional' activities within libraries). This danger has been increased because some recent changes – particularly the coffee bar issue – have been controversial (Self, 2007) and attributable to a small group of named individuals who are seen to be driving unpopular change for political reasons (Cooke, 2007). But it would be wrong to see the bigger question about what should be included in the space occupied by a 21st-century information service as simply a local political issue, and the design of coffee shops in libraries is taken seriously enough for it to be the subject of a peer-reviewed professional journal article (Waxman et al., 2007). Issues like these go to heart of the professional identity of LIS, and some feel strongly that professionalism is at risk from emulating retail and other sectors (Westwood, 2009).

This issue could be seen as just the latest expression of a debate that has been going on for at least half a century to establish just how far the introduction of new technology should be allowed to disrupt the previous model of service provision. The County Librarian of Wiltshire (Hallworth, 1972) railed against what he called the 'defensive smoke screen put out to cover the timorous "custodian" complex: any librarian discussing the possible relevance to his profession of the new media, or worse still advocating its use, was simply labelled "anti-book" – which equated with Philistinism'. He went on to describe the range of what were then known as 'non-book materials' held in the Wiltshire county resource centre – filmstrips, slides, wall-charts, information folders, tapes, framed prints, films, plays, gramophone records, models and specimens, and microfilm. None of this material would raise an eyebrow in the 21st-century library, other than for its interest as an historical curiosity (who now holds any filmstrips as current stock, or has a reel-to-reel tape recorder available?) yet this was clearly a sufficiently heated issue in the 1970s to warrant three pages of the national professional journal. (One library school student wrote to complain that it read like publicity for Wiltshire county libraries, which suggests that it succeeded in raising the county's profile!) We see an ongoing issue that needs appropriate answers if libraries and librarians are not to be condemned, as Hallworth put it almost half a century ago, to a niche in history reserved for stuffed specimens.

Surveys and case studies show us the extent of the current shift away from access to information resources within the confines of the library building. The University of Helsinki is engaged in planning its library service provision from 2012 (Sinikara, 2008); it plans to have finished the transition from 160 library service points – the position in 1994 – to four major campus libraries with the completion of the 'City Campus' library in central Helsinki in 2011–12. A survey instrument of 50 questions in Finnish, Swedish and English was administered in 2005 and again in 2007, covering 5400 participants. It found adverse criticism of the space available for student group work; as Ayris (2008) notes, modern undergraduate courses include new requirements for group working that libraries need to meet. These are poorly met by traditional academic libraries designed solely for individual study. But most striking was the analysis of use of electronic resources by place of use: only 21% of respondents used them in the library, and 49% of respondents used them somewhere off campus.

Findings of this type appear to be also typical of UK and US universities. New and redesigned libraries frequently include suitable space; for example Coventry University's Learning Lounge in the basement of the Lanchester Library combines informal design, refreshments and ready access to virtual resources.

Case study: Coventry University, based on Lanchester Library annual report 2007–8

(www.coventry.ac.uk/cu/external/content/1/c4/19/42/v1238658643/
user/Annual%20Report%20Library%202007-8.pdf)

The library gutted and refurbished a basement area and installed a completely new IT infrastructure using thin client technology, which it launched under the name of the Learning Lounge with space for 126 students. The Lounge has drink and snack machines and students can bring their own food, which they can eat and drink in a cafeteria style area. The area has been popular from the outset; it is now almost permanently close to capacity for most peak study periods. The facility stays open until midnight, although as an experiment 24/7 opening was restored during the examination period to assess demand. This suggested that demand was up on a previous 24/7 facility, and the University is now considering whether to continue this arrangement during future exam times. Accommodation elsewhere in the library has also been upgraded.

The library made a number of other changes around the same time, with the issue desk being renamed the service desk so that it could concentrate on circulation queries, fines payment and reservation collection. Self-service was re-launched as the primary method for the library to issue and accept the return of items. This was a highly successful change, with 71% of items being issued through the self service channel and 40 hours of staff time being saved each week – roughly a full time equivalent member of staff being released for other activities.

Carlson (2001) wrote about the 'deserted library' but it was mainly the reading rooms that were empty in that vision – great use was being made of electronic resources whether from university computer laboratories, students' homes or the wi-fi connection in the local (or indeed not so local – your users could be in another town) Starbucks. He cites another discussion of the coffee-in-libraries issue (Coffman, 1998) and a comment by Robert Seal (librarian of the Texas Christian University) of the irony that Barnes and Noble designed their bookshop coffee bars (which are full on Friday evenings, when campus libraries are not) to have the look and feel of an old-fashioned library. Pomerantz and Marchionini (2007), tracked these trends to predict a transition from libraries as a place of storage for information-containing materials to libraries as a space for users to work individually and collectively, and as a place for social interaction.

As we mentioned earlier, the LibQUAL+® survey instrument

includes five ratings relating to a dimension known as Library as Place: it asks participants to assess library space that inspires study and learning; quiet space for individual work; a comfortable and inviting location; a haven for study, learning or research; and space for group learning and group study. A number of university libraries have published their assessments; we discuss the wider uses of LibQUAL+® in other parts of this book, but in this context we suggest that you will find it useful to examine the comments made by users about their institution's library building and its layout.

The library and its role will continue to evolve. The link between the services provided by librarians and the library building has been severely stretched for some time. We pointed several years ago to helpdesk services being provided on a mutual basis by universities in London and New Zealand, using e-mail to provide user support in the middle of the other institution's night time. This concept has been taken up through initiatives such as Enquire (www.questionpoint. org/crs/servlet/org.oclc.home.TFSRedirect?virtcategory=10836; UK and US public libraries), Chasing the Sun (www.salus.sa.gov.au/ cts/ctsmain.htm; Australian, New Zealand and UK healthcare libraries) and other initiatives mainly based on OCLC's QuestionPoint (www.oclc.org/uk/en/questionpoint/default.htm) software.

What do we conclude from this? We suggest that your strategy to provide user satisfaction needs to take account of the way that your users view the surroundings of the library, and you should be aware in particular of whether the number of physical visitors is increasing or decreasing. Ask yourself and your team a number of questions:

- If visits are going down, is that because more users are taking advantage of your e-facilities, or because they are not finding what they want in the library and are going somewhere else?
- How can you provide new facilities within your budget, or who could help you through sponsorship or a joint venture? (Our publications about outsourcing may help you here.)
- What have you discovered about your users' views and their needs through your surveys, and has anything been done to

address these issues?

- Are you devoting resources to providing facilities that are no longer valued by your users when you could make better use of the funding?

Put yourself in your users' shoes. Answering these questions from their point of view, and some reading of case studies, may make you look at your surroundings in a different light!

Once you're sure about the users, try the exercise again from the point of view of your political patrons, and see whether you can meet the criticism that LIS professionals no longer play to their strengths but emulate other successful sectors such as retailing. Would your answers also convince your sponsor that your service is sound enough to deserve their political backing, and at the same time remain a truly professional service?

Shh, this is a digital library . . .

A 2009 careers article in a national newspaper (Midgley, 2009) highlighted the need for librarians to acquire and apply skills that differ very much from the traditional requirements. (The title of this section is taken from that article and reflects the contrast.) Traditional skills are no longer sufficient in themselves: librarians must also master sophisticated IT and apply advanced information management competencies.

The article went on to emphasize the need for professional training and CPD, sentiments that we endorse (and covered by us in *Your Essential Guide to Career Success* (Pantry and Griffiths, 2003). We believe that CPD is an essential component in delivering continual user satisfaction; staff and managers need to be on top of the technologies and techniques that are constantly evolving. Conference and trade exhibitions offer an alternative to formal training.

Shaping a modern library

We have shown you how the modern library and information service combines many elements that go together in order to provide your users with the service they want. Modern libraries have elements in them that may give concern to some commentators, and we have noted that the decision to install coffee shops may owe as much to the designers of bookshops as it does to the designers of libraries. As we saw earlier on, the concept of the information commons is being increasingly implemented as a means of combining traditional and modern service delivery, and simply as a means of acknowledging that not everything of value to your users appears as print on paper, while many libraries are having to tackle the issue of providing virtual service to a distributed user base.

There remains some question about what exactly constitutes a 'modern' service. Johnson (1994) writes: 'Librarians cannot live in the past, even though some have been guilty of this, but must look to the future and anticipate what another decade may bring.' Modern libraries have to be managed according to modern practices, considering market forces and the current economic climate; but she does not actually define 'modern'. DCMS announced new standards in a document called *Comprehensive, Efficient and Modern Public Libraries*, DCMS, 2000) but apart from the statement that 'Modern public libraries are widespread, popular and of enduring importance to social justice and the maintenance of a democratic society' (which is a comment not a definition), there is no mention of modern libraries other than in the running title above each page. In the section above on politics we cited a number of criteria proposed by the MLA; these are published on their website under the heading 'Shaping a modern library service' – but there's no definition of modern. Rather the proposal seems to be that if all the elements of user satisfaction are met then a modern service will have been created. The supplier Talis considers that modern libraries 'offer an increasing range of products and services' and have to 'increase efficiency and improve user experiences' (Cooper, 2005). And so on. Within the context of a comparative book review Joint (2009b) recommends that 'resources that in the past would have been spent on warehousing expanding collections should nowadays be spent on buying more intensively used digital content and redesigning libraries as open spaces with digital technologies which can facilitate the new learning activities associated with the electronic campus', which is in effect defining digital resources as a key element of a modern library – but as Kova (2008) suggests, there is something about print on paper that will not go away, as almost 100% of printed books are made into e-books during the printing process and a library could therefore consist entirely of PDF copies – something that is clearly not happening even though we are starting to see libraries lending e-books and major booksellers selling them.

In the context of user satisfaction, a modern library consists (we suggest) of the perfect balance of virtual and printed resources housed in a building designed and constructed to deliver those resources in optimum conditions, managed and facilitated by professional staff who are activists in their profession and who take full advantage of continuing professional development opportunities for the benefit of the users and sponsors of their service. This definition is full – and it is challenging.

Challenges for the future

The LIS and knowledge and information management (KIM) profession faces many challenges as a result of the changes that we have been describing. Returning to the thesis that sparked our concern to put this book together, the main challenge is that the coming generation of users ('Generation Y', 'Google Generation', etc.) has different expectations and different ways of working that mean that it will be left unsatisfied by current services. But this major issue hides the smaller and subtler changes that all users undergo as they find out more about what is on offer (and who says they cannot talk directly to suppliers?). Traditional-seeming workplaces are populated by new-style users – for example lawyers whose university studies were supported by access to electronic resources, decision makers who get their information from news websites, and people who record their personal and professional lives in blogs and on social networking sites and expect to use these facilities to support their work activities.

The challenge goes wider than new means of information access; for example Generation Y users have different (and not always compliant) ideas about intellectual property use and rights. They view rather than read so have a preference for information presented in graphic form even if that is less accurate than an explanation in text. They have lower levels of digital and information literacy than might have been expected. There is much more to learn before we know enough about user requirements to be able to deliver the service users need – which is why a three-year research project had just been commissioned as this book was going to press in order to provide detailed information to back up the broad findings of the Google Generation study by JISC (2008) (Venkatraman, 2009). Part of the CPD that each of us should undertake will be to keep up to date with the progress and findings of the new study.

So the story of user satisfaction and the delivery of high quality service to LIS users has more many chapters to be written, and the future will be exciting and challenging. But is the information profession geared up for this and are the professional bodies (such as CILIP: the Chartered Institute of Information Professionals, in the UK) ready to lead the way – or are we going to let others show us what should be done to give users the LIS services they want?

Appendix 1
Reading list and references

Chapter 1 Why this book?

CIBER (2008) *Information Behaviour of the Researcher of the Future [executive summary]*, University College London, www.ucl.ac.uk/infostudies/research/ciber/downloads/ggexecutive.pdf.

Nicholas, D. and Rowlands, I. (eds) (2008) *Digital Consumers: reshaping the information professions*, Facet Publishing, ISBN 978-1-85604-651-0.

OCLC (2006) *College Students' Perceptions of the Libraries and Information Resources: a report to the OCLC membership*, Online Computer Library Center.

Shirky, C. (2008) *Every Piece of Information is a Latent Community: Online 2008, address.* Given 2 December 2008 at Olympia Grand Hall, London, UK, http://theshiftedlibrarian.com/archives/2008/12/02/clay-shirkey-online-information-keynote.html.

Verlejs, J. (1988) *Information Seeking: basing services on users' behaviour*, McFarland, ISBN 978-0-89950254-0.

Chapter 2 Understanding users – the what, why, where, when, how and who

Bawden, D. and Vilar, P. (2006) Digital Libraries: to meet or manage user expectations, *Aslib Proceedings*, 58 (4), 346–54.

Björneborn, L. (2006) *Libraries as Integrative Interfaces –tracking users' information interaction in context*, Royal School of Library and Information Science, Copenhagen, Denmark, Working paper, version 3.
This working paper outlines an ongoing exploratory research project concerned with how users interact with the physical interior of public libraries.

CIBER (2008) *Information Behaviour of the Researcher of the Future [executive summary]*, University College London, www.ucl.ac.uk/infostudies/research/ciber/downloads/ggexecutive. pdf.

Curzon, S. C. (2006) *Managing Change: a how-to-do-it manual for librarians*, Facet Publishing, ISBN 978-1-85604-601-5.

Dempsey, L. (2006) The (Digital) Library Environment: ten years after, *Ariadne*, **46** (February), www.ariadne.ac.uk/issue46/dempsey/.

Dempsey, L. (2008, 2009) Always On: libraries in a world of permanent connectivity. In Needham, G. and Ally, M. (eds) *M-libraries: libraries on the move to provide virtual access*, Facet Publishing, xxv–lii; slightly revised version published in *First Monday*, **14** (1–5), January 2009, http://firstmonday.org/htbin/cgiwrap/bin/ojs/index.php/fm/article/ viewArticle/2291/2070.

Dorner, D. G. and Gorman, G. E. (2010) *Analysing What Your Users Need: a guide for librarians and information managers*, Facet Publishing, ISBN 978-1-85604-484-4 (in press).

Ealing Library and Information Service (1995) [*Evidence to the DNH Public Library Review*], http://panizzi.shef.ac.uk/library-review/london/ealin.html.

Frand, J. (2006) The Information Mindset: changes in students and implications for higher education, *EDUCAUSE Review*, March/April, 15.

Hyams, E. (2001) Nursing the Evidence: The Royal College of Nursing information strategy, *Library Association Record*, **103** (12), 747–9.

Large, A. (2006) Children, Teenagers and the Web, *Annual Review of Information, Science and Technology,* **39** (1), 347–92.

OCLC (2006) *College Students' Perceptions of the Libraries and Information Resources: a report to the OCLC membership,* Online Computer Library Center.

Pantry, S. (ed.) (1999) *Building Community Information Networks: strategies and experiences,* Library Association Publishing, ISBN 978-1-85604-337-3.

Pantry, S. and Griffiths, P. (1998) *Becoming a Successful Intrapreneur: a practical guide to creating an innovative information service,* Library Association Publishing, ISBN 978-1-85604-292-5.

Pantry, S. and Griffiths, P. (2000) *Developing a Successful Service Plan,* Library Association Publishing, ISBN 978-1-85604-392-2.

Pantry, S. and Griffiths, P. (2001) *The Complete Guide to Preparing and Implementing Service Level Agreements,* 2nd edn, Library Association Publishing, ISBN 978-1-85604-410-6.

Pantry, S. and Griffiths, P. (2002) *Creating a Successful E-information Service,* Facet Publishing, ISBN 978-1-85604-442-4.

Pantry, S. and Griffiths, P. (2003) *Creating a Successful E-information Service* (North American edn, edited by W. Oldfield), Scarecrow Press, Inc. (Rowman & Littlefield, Inc.), ISBN 0-81084-778-7.

Pantry, S. and Griffiths, P. (2004) *Managing Outsourcing in Library and Information Services,* Facet Publishing, ISBN 978-1-85604-543-8.

Pantry, S. and Griffiths, P. (2005) *Setting up a Library and Information Service from Scratch,* Facet Publishing, ISBN 978-1-85604-558-2.

Ponsford, B. C. and van Duinkerken, W. (2007) User Expectations in the Time of Google: usability testing of federated searching, *Internet Reference Services Quarterly,* **12** (1/2), 159–78.

Rowlands, I. and Fieldhouse, M. (2007) *Trends in Scholarly Information Behaviour: work package 1,* British Library and JISC,

www.jisc.ac.uk/media/documents/programmes/reres/
ggworkpackagei.pdf.

Rowley, J. (2001) JISC Behaviour Monitoring and Evaluation
Framework, *Ariadne*, **30**,
www.ariadne.ac.uk/issue30/jisc/intro.html.
Jenny Rowley, JISC Scientific Advisor, reports on a JISC research
framework that monitors and maps the development of user
behaviour with electronic information resources in UK higher
education.

Royal College of Nursing (2005) *The Information Needs of Nurses;
summary report of an RCN survey*, RCN,
www.rcn.org.uk/_data/assets/pdf_file/0010/78670/002780.pdf.

Chapter 3 What is the current knowledge about your users and their needs – is it really predictable?

Akeroyd, J. (2001) The Management of Change in Electronic
Libraries, *IFLA Journal*, **27** (2), 70–3.

Bailey, D. R. and Tierney, B. G. (2008) *Transforming Library Service
through Information Commons: case studies for the digital age*,
American Library Association.

Barrett, A. (2005) The Information-seeking Habits of Graduate
Student Researchers in Humanities, *Journal of Academic
Librarianship*, **31** (4), 324–31.

Bawden, D. (1986) Information Systems and the Stimulation of
Creativity, *Journal of Information Science*, **12**, 203–16.

Biblarz, D., Bosch, S. and Sugnet, C. (2001) *Guide to Library User
Needs Assessment for Integrated Information Resource*, Scarecrow.

Bradley, M., Hemminger, D. L., Vaughan, K. T. L. and Adams, S. J.
(2007) Information Seeking Behavior of Academic Scientists,
*Journal of the American Society for Information Science and
Technology*, **58** (14) 2205–25.
The information seeking behaviour of academic scientists is being
transformed by the availability of electronic resources for
searching, retrieving and reading scholarly materials. A census

survey was conducted of academic science researchers at the University of North Carolina at Chapel Hill to capture their current information-seeking behaviour. Nine hundred and two subjects (26%) completed responses to a 15-minute web-based survey. The survey questions were designed to quantify the transition to electronic communications and how this affects different aspects of information seeking. Significant changes in information-seeking behaviour were found, including increased reliance on web-based resources, fewer visits to the library, and almost entirely electronic communication of information. The results can guide libraries and other information service organizations as they adapt to meet the needs of today's information searchers. Simple descriptive statistics are reported for the individual questions. Additionally, analysis of results is broken down by basic science and medical science departments. The survey tool and protocol used in this study have been adopted for use in a nationwide survey of the information-seeking behaviour of academic scientists.

Brenneise, H. and Marks, R. (2001) Creating a State-Wide Virtual Health Library, *Online Information Review*, **25** (2), 115–20.

Bury Times (2009) CAB Debt Clinic Launched in Bury for Crisis Advice, *Bury Times*, 14 February, www.thisislancashire.co.uk/news/burytimes/4118961.CAB_ debt_clinic_launched_in_Bury_for_crisis_advice/.

Campbell, D. E. and Shlechter, T. M. (1979) Library Design Influences on User Behavior and Satisfaction, *Library Quarterly*, **49** (1), 26–41.

Casey, M. E. and Savastinuk, L. C. (2006) Library 2.0: service for the next-generation library, *Library Journal*, **14** (1 September), www.libraryjournal.com/article/CA6365200.html.

Chi, M. T. H. (1997) Quantifying Qualitative Analyses of Verbal Data: a practical guide, *Journal of the Learning Sciences*, **6** (3), 271–315.

CIBER (2008) *Information Behaviour of the Researcher of the Future [executive summary]*, University College London,

www.ucl.ac.uk/infostudies/research/ciber/downloads/ggexecutive.
pdf.

Crane, D. (1972) *Invisible Colleges: diffusion of knowledge in
scientific communities,* University of Chicago Press.

Davitt M. P. (1999) Library Resources and Services: a cross-
disciplinary survey of faculty and graduate students' use and
satisfaction, *Journal of Academic Librarianship*, 25 (5), 354–66.

D'Elia, G. (1980) The Development and Testing of a Conceptual
Model of Public Library User Behavior, *Library Quarterly*, 50, 4
(October), 410.
    Reports results of a study that tested a hierarchical model that
considers public library use as a function of the user's individual
characteristics, awareness of library services, perceived
accessibility of the library, perceived ease of use of the library,
and use of other nonpublic libraries.

De Rosa, C. et al. (2003) *Perceptions of Libraries and Information
Resources: a report to the OCLC membership,* Online Computer
Library Center, www.oclc.org/uk/en/reports/pdfs/Percept_all.pdf.

Fisher, K. E., Erdelez, S. and McKechnie, E. F. (eds) (2005)
Theories of Information Behaviour: a researcher's guide,
Information Today.

Fontana, A. and Frey, J. H. (1995) Interviewing: the art of science.
In Denzin, N. K. and Lincoln, Y. (eds), *Handbook of Qualitative
Research*, Sage, 361–73.

Ford, N. (1999) Information Retrieval and Creativity: towards
support for the original thinker, *Journal of Documentation*, 55
(5), 528–42.

Foster, A. and Ford, N. (2003) Serendipity and Information Seeking:
an empirical study, *Journal of Documentation*, 59 (3), 321–40.

Friedlander, A. (2002) Dimensions and Use of Scholarly
Information Environment. Introduction to a data set assembled
by the Digital Library Federation and Outsell. Inc.,
www.clir.org/pubs/reports/pub110/contents.html.

George, C., Bright, A., Hurlbert, T. and Linke, E. C. (2006)
Scholarly Use of Information: graduate students' information

seeking behaviour, *Information Research*, **11** (4),
http://InformationR.net/ir/11–4/paper272.html.

Given, L. M. and Leckie, G. J. (2003) 'Sweeping' the Library:
mapping the social activity space of the public library, *Library &
Information Science Research*, **25** (4), 365–85.

Goodall, D. L. (1989) *Browsing in Public Libraries*, Library and
Information Statistics Unit, Loughborough University of
Technology.

Goodman, D. (2002) A Year Without Print at Princeton, and What
We Plan Next, *Learned Publishing*, **15** (1), January, 43–50.

Gorman, G. E. and Clayton, P. (2004) *Qualitative Research for the
Information Professional: a practical handbook,* 2nd edn, Facet
Publishing, ISBN 978-1-85604-472-1.

Griffiths J.-M. (1998) Why the Web is Not a Library. In Hawkins B.
L. and Battin P. (eds), *The Mirage of Continuity: reconfiguring
academic information resources for the 21st century*, Council on
Library and Information Resources and Association of American
Universities, 229–46.

Haglund, L. and Olsson, P. (2008) The Impact on University
Libraries of Changes in Information Behavior Among Academic
Researchers: a multiple case study, *Journal of Academic
Librarianship*, **34** (1) 52–9.

Harley, B., Dreger, M. and Knobloch, P. (2001) The Postmodern
Condition: students, the web and academic library services,
Reference Services Review, **29** (1), 23–32.

Heinstrom, J. (2005) Fast Surfing, Broad Scanning and Deep
Diving: the influence of personality and study approach on
students' information-seeking behavior, *Journal of
Documentation*, **61** (2), 228–47.

Hepworth, M. (2007) Knowledge of Information Behaviour and Its
Relevance to the Design of People-Centred Information Products
and Services, *Journal of Documentation,* **63** (1), 33–56.

Ingwersen, P. and Järvelin, K. (2005) *The Turn: integration of
information seeking and retrieval in context*, Springer.

International Federation of Library Associations (2005) *Meeting*

User Needs: a checklist for best practice, produced by Section 8 – Public Libraries Section of IFLA, revised July 2008. Participants in compiling this checklist: Assumpta Bailac [and others], www.ifla.org/VII/s8/proj/Mtg_UN-Checklist.pdf.
Includes links to a number of survey instruments and reports on their use in libraries in several countries.

Law, D. (1997) Parlour Games: the real nature of the internet, *Serials*, **10** (2), 195–201.

Lorenzen, M. (2001) The Land of Confusion? High school students and their use of the world wide web for research, *Research Strategies*, **18** (2), 151–63.

Lushington, N. (2002) *Libraries Designed for Users: a 21st century guide*, Neal-Schuman.

Malenfant, C. (2006) The Information Commons as a Collaborative Workspace, *Reference Services Review*, **34** (2), 279–86.

Mansourian, Y. and Ford, N. (2007) Search Persistence and Failure on the Web: a 'bounded rationality' and 'satisficing' analysis, *Journal of Documentation*, **63** (5), 680–701.

Merton, R. K. and Barber, E. G. (2004) *The Travels and Adventures of Serendipity: a study in historical semantics and the sociology of science*, Princeton University Press.

Museums, Libraries and Archives Council (2006) *Community Engagement in Public Libraries: a toolkit for public library staff*, MLA and CSV Consulting.

Muet, F. (1999) Services et Revues Electroniques dans l'Enseignement Supérieur: synthèse de quelques enquêtes récentes sur les usages, *Bulletin des Bibliothèques de France*, **44** (5), 18–23.

Online Computer Library Center (2002) *How Academic Librarians Can Influence Students' Web-Based Information Choices*, www5.oclc.org/downloads/community/informationhabits.pdf.

Nicholas, D. et al. (2006) The Information Seeking Behaviour of the Users of Digital Scholarly Journals, *Information Processing and Management: an international journal*, **42** (5), 1345–65.

Parker, N. (2001) Student Learning as Information Behaviour:

exploring assessment task processes, *Information Research*, **6** (2), http://InformationR.net/ir/6–2/ws5.html.

Patton, M. Q. (1990) *Qualitative Evaluation and Research Methods*, Sage.

Pickard, A. J. (2007) *Research Methods in Information*, Facet Publishing, ISBN 978-1-85604-545-2.

Pinfield, S. (2001) Managing Electronic Library Services: current issues in UK higher education institutions, *Ariadne*, **29**, www.ariadne.ac.uk/issue29/pinfield/.

Prensky, M. (2001) Digital Natives, Digital Immigrants, *On the Horizon*, **9** (1), 1–6, www.markprensky.com and archived at www.webcitation.org/5eBDYI5Uw.

Reddy, M. C. and Jansen, B. J. (2008) A Model for Understanding Information Behavior in Context: a study of two healthcare teams, *Information Processing & Management*, **44** (1), 256–73.

Rowlands, I. and Nicholas, D. (2008) Understanding Information Behaviour: how do students and faculty find books?, *Journal of Academic Librarianship*, **34** (1), 3–15.

Sadler, E. and Given, L. M. (2007) Affordance Theory: a framework for graduate students information behavior, *Journal of Documentation*, **63** (1), 115–41.

Sherman, S. (2008) *A User-centered Evaluation of the North Carolina State University Libraries Learning Commons*, a Master's paper for the MS in LS degree, April, http://etd.ils.unc.edu:8080/dspace/bitstream/1901/540/1/ stephensherman.pdf.

Slater, M. (1981) *The Neglected Resource: non-usage of library and information services in industry and commerce*, Aslib, ISBN 978-0-85142-145-2.

Spink, A. (2004) Multitasking Information Behavior and Information Task Switching: an exploratory study, *Journal of Documentation*, **60** (4), 336–51.

Steinerova, J. and Susol, J. (2005) Library Users in Human Information Behaviour, *Online Information Review*, **29** (2), 139–56.

Talja, S. (2002) Information Sharing in Academic Communities: types and levels of collaboration, *New Review of Information Behaviour Research*, www.info.uta.fi/talja/Taljaisic2002_konv.pdf.

Thorny Hlynsdottir and Thora Gylfadottir (2004) Remote Document Supply in Iceland Before and After Nationwide Access to 8000 E-journals: the story so far . . ., *Interlending and Document Supply*, **32** (2), 70–9.

Thora Gylfadottir and Thorny Hlynsdottir (2006) Iceland: the story continues . . . of nationwide access to e-journals, *Interlending and Document Supply*, **34** (1), 9–14.

Uçak, N. Ö. (2004) User Studies in Turkey: an evaluation of dissertations, *Information Development*, **20** (2), 122–9.
Presents a picture of the recent situation of user studies in Turkey and makes an evaluation. The research population encompassed theses completed from 1958 to 2002 in departments of librarianship or information management and other departments in Turkish universities. A total of 33 dissertations were investigated in the year when they were completed, the department where they were conducted, research methods and data collection techniques and type of research – whether system oriented or user oriented. The findings reveal that user studies in Turkey are usually evaluated in relation to the information centre, that the number of studies increased in the last ten years, and that users in the field of education (students, academicians) are preferred as the focus of study. The theses usually describe the existing situation and problems. Quantitative methods are the most frequently used. The study also makes some suggestions in the light of the findings.

Underhill, P. (1999) *Why We Buy: the science of shopping*, Simon & Schuster.

Urquhart, C., Lonsdale, R., Thomas, R., Spink, S., Yeoman, A., Armstrong, C. and Fenton, R. (2003) Uptake and Use of Electronic Information Services: trends in UK higher education from the JUSTEIS project, *Program*, **37** (3), 167–80, http://cadair.aber.ac.uk/dspace/handle/2160/191.

Van Andel, P. (1994) Anatomy of the Unsought Finding: serendipity: origin, history, domains, traditions, appearances, patterns and programmability, *British Journal for the Philosophy of Science*, **45** (2), 631–48.

Van de Stadt, I. (2007) Going E-only: all Icelandic citizens are hooked (interview with Solveig Thosteinsdottir), *Library Connect*, **5** (1), 2.

Vezzosi, M. (2008) *Linking Teaching and Learning: a longitudinal approach to the assessment of information literacy*, http://edoc.hu-berlin.de/conferences/bobcatsss2008/vezzosi-monica-202/PDF/vezzosi.pdf.

Wallis, J. (2003) Information-saturated Yet Ignorant: information mediation as social empowerment in the knowledge economy, *Library Review*, **52** (8), 369–72.

Webb, J., Gannon-Leary, P. and Bent, M. (2007) *Providing Effective Library Services for Research*, Facet Publishing, ISBN 978-1-85604-589-6.

Wellner, P., Mackay, W. and Gold, R. (2003) Special Issue on Computer Augmented Environments: back to the real world, *Communications of the ACM*, **36** (7), 24–6.

Wilkie, S. (2006) Community Engagement at Topping Fold: MLA's strategy, *Public Library Journal*, Spring, 13–16.

Wilson, T. D. (1999) Models in Information Behaviour Research, *Journal of Documentation*, **55** (3), 249–70.

Chapter 4 Great expectations: how LIS professionals can manage and train users

Beatty, S. and White, P. (2005) Information Commons: models for e-learning and the integration of learning, *Journal of eLiteracy*, 2, 2–14, www.jelit.org/52/01/JeLit_Paper_16.pdf.

Bradley, P. (2007) *How to Use Web 2.0 in Your Library*, Facet Publishing, ISBN 978-1-85604-607-7.

Darlington, J., Finney, A. and Pearce, A. (2003) Domesday Redux: the rescue of the BBC Domesday Project videodiscs, *Ariadne*, **36**, www.ariadne.ac.uk/issue36/tna/.

Flanders, D. F. and Hedges, M. (eds) (2010) *The Complete Guide to Repositories*, Facet Publishing, ISBN 978-1-85604-676-3 (in press).

Jacquesson, A. (2000) De la Difficulté à Utiliser les Bibliothèques Numériques, *Bulletin d'Information* (Association des Bibliothécaires de France), 188, 3e trimestre, www.abf.asso.fr/IMG/pdf/n188_2.pdf.

Lee, S. D. and Boyle, F. (2004) *Building an Electronic Resource Collection: a practical guide*, Facet Publishing, ISBN 978-1-85604-531-5.

McCauley, C. (2007) The Library in Second Life: presentation to JIBS workshop *Is Library 2.0 a Trivial Pursuit?*, www.jibs.ac.uk/events/workshops/web2.0/second-life.ppt.

Pasenen, I. and Muhonen, A. (2002) *Library in Your Pocket, Annual International Association of Technology University Librarians conference, 23rd, Kansas City, Missouri*, www.iatul.org/doclibrary/public/Conf_Proceeedings/2002/muhonen.t.

Secker, J. (2008) *Libraries and Facebook*, University of London Centre for Distance Education, http://clt.lse.ac.uk/Projects/Case_Study_Five_report.pdf.

Sidorko, P. E. and Yang, T. T. (2009) Refocusing for the Future: meeting user expectations in a digital age, *Library Management*, 30 (1/2), 6–24.

Slater, M. (1981) *The Neglected Resource: non-usage of library and information services in industry and commerce*, Aslib, ISBN 978-08514-214-52.

Sokoloff, J. (2009) International Libraries on Facebook, *Journal of Web Librarianship*, 3 (1), 75–80.

Special Libraries Association (2003) *Competencies for Information Professionals of the 21st Century* (rev. edn), www.sla.org/PDFs/Competencies2003.pdf.

Wilkie, S. (2006) Community Engagement, Topping Fold and MLA's approach, *Public Library Journal*, 21, Spring, 13–16.

Zimmerer, T. W., Scarborough, N. M. and Wilson, D. (2007) *Essentials of Entrepreneurship and Small Business Management*, Pearson Education.

Web resource

People's Network (in the UK's public libraries) to cover the essential work of those being trained, www.peoplesnetwork.gov.uk.

Chapter 5 Using information about past user behaviour

Accesscable.net (1997) *Survey Tips: how to write a good survey questionnaire*, www.accesscable.net/~infopoll/tips.htm.

Bryant, J., Matthews, G. and Walton, G. (2009) Academic Libraries and Social and Learning Space: a case study of Loughborough University Library, *Journal of Librarianship and Information Science*, **41** (1), March, 7–18.
A case study looking at collaborative study, individual study, social space, intrusions and interruptions, use of technology, diversity, library staff and library materials and spatial organization.

Creaser, C., Maynard, S. and White, S. (2007) *LISU Annual Library Statistics 2006: featuring trend analysis of UK public and academic libraries 1995–2005*, Library and Information Statistics Unit.

Dillman, D. A., Smyth, J. D. and Christian, L. H. (2008) *Internet, Mail and Mixed-Mode Surveys: the tailored design method*, 3rd edn, Wiley.

Library Research Service (2003) *Library User Surveys on the Web*, Library Research Service, www.lrs.org/usersurveys.php.

Pantry, S. and Griffiths, P. (1998) *Becoming a Successful Intrapreneur: a practical guide to creating an innovative information service*, Library Association Publishing,

ISBN 978-1-85604-292-5.

Pantry, S. and Griffiths, P. (2000) *Developing a Successful Service Plan*, Library Association Publishing, ISBN 978-1-85604-392-2.

Pantry, S. and Griffiths, P. (2002) *Creating a Successful E-information Service*, Facet Publishing, ISBN 978-1-85604-442-4.

Pantry, S. and Griffiths, P. (2003) *Creating a Successful E-Information Service* (North American edn, edited by W. Oldfield), Scarecrow Press, Inc. (Rowman & Littlefield, Inc.), ISBN 0-81084-778-7.

Pantry, S. and Griffiths, P. (2005) *Setting up a Library and Information Service from Scratch*, Facet Publishing, ISBN 978-1-85604-558-2.

Plosker, G. (2002) Conducting User Surveys: an ongoing information imperative, *Online*, **26** (5), September/October, 64–9, www.infotoday.com/online/sep02/Plosker.htm. Useful summary of classic approach to library user surveys – but its limitations indicated by the comment that you can use the data as a management tool in terms of defining approaches to meet defined needs – what about discovering so far undefined needs and meeting those?

Sue, V. M. and Ritter, L. A. (2007) *Conducting Online Surveys*, new edn, Sage.

TechSoup (2008) *Use Online Surveys to Get the Feedback You Need*. TechSoup – the technology place for non-profits, 25 August, www.techsoup.org/learningcenter/internet/page5048.cfm.

Chapter 6 Making the most of knowing your users

Björneborn, L. (2006) *Libraries as Integrative Interfaces – tracking users' information interaction in context*, Royal School of Library and Information Science, Copenhagen.

Boran, M. (2008) UCD Library Targets FaceBook, Silicon Republic [website], 18 July, www.siliconrepublic.com/news/article/11055/.

Camber, R. (2007) 'Little Fat Library Man' Ridiculed in Students'

Facebook Bullying Campaign, *Daily Mail*, 24 July, www.dailymail.co.uk/news/article-470610/Little-fat-library-man-ridiculed-students-Facebook-bullying-campaign.html.

Chim, W. (2007) The Quest for Excellence: one library's experience, *Library Management*, **28** (6/7), 323–36.

CIBER (2008) *Information Behaviour of the Researcher of the Future [executive summary]*, University College London, www.ucl.ac.uk/infostudies/research/ciber/downloads/ggexecutive.pdf.

Connaway, L. S. (2008) Make Way for the Millennials, *NextSpace*, **10** (October), 18–19.

Connaway, L. S. et al. (2008) Sense-Making and Synchronicity: information-seeking and communication behaviors of millennials and baby boomers, *Libri*, **58** (2), 123–35.

Conyers, A. (2004) E-measures: developing statistical measures for electronic information services, *Vine*, **34** (4), 148–53.

Corrall, S. (2000) *Strategic Management of Information Services: a planning handbook*, Aslib/IMI, ISBN 0-85142-346-9.

Corrall, S. (2003) Strategic Planning in Academic Libraries. In Drake, M. (ed.), *Encyclopedia of Library and Information Science*, 2nd edn, Dekker, 2742–54.

Creaser, C., Davies, J. E. and Wisdom, S. (2002) Accessible, Open and Inclusive: how visually impaired people view library and information services and agencies, *Journal of Documentation*, **34** (4) (December), 207–14.

Curzon, S. C. (2006) *Managing Change: a how-to-do-it manual for librarians*, Facet Publishing, ISBN 978-1-85604-601-5.

Dempsey, L. (2008, 2009) Always On: libraries in a world of permanent connectivity. In Needham, G. and Ally, M. (eds), M-libraries: libraries on the move to provide virtual access, Facet Publishing, 2008, xxv–lii; slightly revised version published in *First Monday*, **14** (1–5), January 2009, http://firstmonday.org/htbin/cgiwrap/bin/ojs/index.php/fm/article/view/2291/2070.

De Saez, E. E. (2002) *Marketing Concepts for Libraries and*

Information Services, Facet Publishing, ISBN 978-1-85604-426-4.

Farkas, M. (2007) *Social Software in Libraries: building collaboration, communication, and community online*, Information Today.

Graham, J. M., Faix, A. and Hartman, L. (2009) Crashing the Facebook Party: one library's experience in the student domain, *Library Review*, **58** (3), 228–36.

Griffiths, P. (2009) Five Things that Government Librarians Can Teach the Profession, *Government Libraries Journal*, **19** (2) (June), 9–12, www.cilip.org.us/NR/rdonlyres/6500D849-89A8-4DAF-9C09-3E5C87661DF2/0/GLIG_Journal_0906.pdf.

Harriman, J. H. P. (2008) *Creating Your Library's Business Plan: a how-to-do it manual with samples on CD-ROM*, Facet Publishing, ISBN 978-1-85604-656-5.

Hart, K. (1999) *Putting Marketing Ideas into Action*, Library Association Publishing.

Higher Education in a Web 2.0 World: report of an independent committee of enquiry into the impact on higher education of students' widespread use of Web 2.0 technologies (2009) (Chairman, Professor Sir David Melville), Joint Information Systems Committee, www.jisc.ac.uk/media/documents/publications/heweb20rptv1.pdf.

Hildebrand, I. (2003) Service Please!: rethinking public library websites, *Library Review*, **52** (6), 268–77.

Kann-Christensen, N. and Andersen, J. (2009) Developing the Library: between efficiency, accountability and forms of recognition, *Journal of Documentation*, **65** (2), 208–22.

Kendrick, T. (2006) *Developing Strategic Marketing Plans that Really Work*, Facet Publishing, ISBN 978-1-85604-548-3.

McIntyre, A. and Nicolle, J. (2008) Biblioblogging: blogs for library communication, *Electronic Library*, **26** (5) 683–94.

Melling, M. and Little, J. (2002) *Building a Successful Customer-Service Culture: a guide for library and information managers*, Facet Publishing, ISBN 978-1-85604-449-3.

Nielsen, H. J. (2009) Library Communication Outside a Library

Context: instant messaging as a library service, *New Library World*, **110** (5), May, 237–48.

Oldman, C. (1977) Marketing Library and Information Services: the strengths and weaknesses of a marketing approach, *European Journal of Marketing*, **11** (6), 460–74.

Pan, R. (2007) UCD Library – Getting Out There! *SCONUL Focus*, **40**, (Spring), 26–30, www.sconul.ac.uk/publications/newsletter/40/9.pdf.

Pantry, S. and Griffiths, P. (1998) *Becoming a Successful Intrapreneur: a practical guide to creating an innovative information service*, Library Association Publishing, ISBN 978-1-85604-292-5.

Pantry, S. and Griffiths, P. (2000) *Developing a Successful Service Plan*, Library Association Publishing, ISBN 978-1-85604-392-2.

Pantry, S. and Griffiths, P. (2001) *The Complete Guide to Preparing and Implementing Service Level Agreements*, 2nd edn, Library Association Publishing, ISBN 978-1-85604-410-6.

Pantry, S. and Griffiths, P. (2002) *Creating a Successful E-Information Service*, Facet Publishing, ISBN 978-1-85604-442-4.

Pantry, S. and Griffiths, P. (2003) *Creating a Successful E-Information Service* (North American edn, edited by W. Oldfield), Scarecrow Press, Inc. (Rowman & Littlefield, Inc.), ISBN 0-8108-4778-7.

Pantry, S. and Griffiths, P. (2004) *Managing Outsourcing in Library and Information Services*, Facet Publishing, ISBN 978-1-85604-543-8.

Pantry, S. and Griffiths, P. (2005) *Setting up a Library and Information Service from Scratch*, Facet Publishing, ISBN 978-1-85604-558-2.

Rowse, M. (ed.) (2003) Individual Article Supply: some strategic decisions, *Interlending and Document*, **31** (2), 86–93.

Sidorko, P. E. and Yang, T. T. (2009) Refocusing for the Future: meeting user expectations in a digital age, *Library Management*, **30** (1/2), 6–24.

Singh, R. (2009a) Mind the Gap: unlocking the relationship

between market-orientation and service performance, *Library Review*, **58** (1), 28–43.

Singh, R. (2009b) Does Your Library Have a Marketing Culture? Implications for service providers, *Library Management*, **30** (3), 117–37.

Why are some libraries more market-oriented than others? This paper seeks to answer this question by examining the pertinent issues underlying the marketing culture of Finnish research libraries and the library management's awareness of modern marketing theories and practices.

Taylor, K. and Corrall, S. (2007) Personalized Service? Changing the role of the government librarian, *Journal of Information Science*, **33** (3), 298–314.

Williams, L. (2006) Making 'E' Visible: to draw patrons past the Googles of the world, we need to revolutionize how electronic resources are promoted, *Library Journal*, **23**, www.libraryjournal.com/article/CA6341888.html.

Woodward, J. (2004) *Creating the Customer-Driven Library: building on the bookstore model*, American Library Association, ISBN 978-0-8389-0888-4.

Academic libraries are going through what may be the most difficult period in their history. With more and more scholarly content available online and accessible almost anywhere, where does the traditional brick and mortar library fit in? In this book Jeannette Woodward attacks these and other pressing issues facing today's academic librarians. Her trailblazing strategies centre on keeping the customer's point of view in focus at all times to help you:

- integrate technology to meet today's student and faculty needs
- revaluate the role and function of library service desks
- implement staffing strategies to match customer expectations
- create new and effective promotional materials.

Librarians are now faced with marketing to a generation of

students who log on rather than walk in and this cutting-edge book supplies the tools needed to keep customers coming through the door.

Web resource

www.librarysuortstaff.com/strategicplan.html.

Chapter 7 Keeping track of changes in what users want

Barton, J. (2004) Measurement, Management and the Digital Library, *Library Review*, 53 (3), 138–41.

Bridges, L. M. (2008) Who is Not Using the Library? A comparison of undergraduate disciplines and library use, *Portal: Libraries and the Academy*, 8 (2), 187–96,
http://muse.jhu.edu/journals/portal_libraries_and_the_academy/v008/8.2bridges.html.

Connaway, L. S. (2008) Make Way for the Millennials, *NextSpace*, 10 (October), 18–19.
Looks at the information-seeking habits of the Millennial generation – people currently 14–28 years old – and how libraries can match their information services with those habits. Also known as Generation Y, the Net Generation, or Echo Boomers, this group of approximately 76 million people have been described as thinking and processing information fundamentally differently from their predecessors. Millennials cannot remember life without computers or mobile phones, tend to be impatient, pay less attention to spelling and grammar, and have a low tolerance for complex searching.

Cox, J., Martinez, E. and Quinlan, K. B. (2008) Blogs and the Corporation: managing the risk, reaping the benefit, *Journal of Business Strategy*, 29 (3), 4–12.

Ford, G. (2002) Strategic Uses of Evaluation and Performance Measurement, *Proceedings of the 4th Northumbria International*

Conference on Performance Measurement in Libraries and Information Services, Association of Research Libraries, Washington, DC, 12–16 August 2001.

Haglund, L. O. P. (2008) The Impact on University Libraries of Changes in Information Behavior Among Academic Researchers: a multiple case study, *Journal of Academic Librarianship*, **34** (1), 3–15.

To better understand the information needs of young university researchers, an observational study was performed at three universities in Stockholm, Sweden. The observations revealed that most of the researchers used Google for everything, that they were confident that they could manage on their own, and that they relied heavily on immediate access to electronic information. They had very little contact with the library, and little knowledge about the value librarian competence could add. One important conclusion of the project is that librarians have to leave the library building and start working in the research environment, as well as putting some thought into the fact that library use is considered complicated, but Google (etc.) is easy. The findings of this project will influence changes in library services in both the near and a more distant future.

Hyams, E. (2001) Nursing the Evidence: the Royal College of Nursing information strategy, *Library Association Record*, **103** (12), 747–9.

Nielsen, J. (1999) *Designing Web Usability: the practice of simplicity*, USA, New Raiders.

McClure, R. and Clink, K. (2009) How Do You Know That?: an investigation of student research practices in the digital age, *Portal: Libraries and the Academy*, **9** (1) (January), 115–32.

This study investigates the types of sources that English composition students use in their research essays. Unlike previous studies, this project pairs an examination of source citations with deeper analysis of source use, and both are discussed in relation to responses gathered in focus groups with participating students and teachers. The researchers examine how students negotiate locating and using source material, particularly online sources, in terms of timeliness, authority and bias. The researchers report on how teachers struggle to introduce these concepts and how students fail to perceive authority and bias in their sources.

McKnight, S. (ed.) (2010) *Envisioning Future Library Services: initiatives, ideas and challenges*, Facet Publishing, ISBN 978-1-85604-691-6 (in press).

Pantry, S. and Griffiths, P. (1998) *Becoming a Successful Intrapreneur: a practical guide to creating an innovative information service*, Library Association Publishing, ISBN 978-1-85604-292-5.

Plum, T. et al. (2008) Measuring the Impact of Networked Electronic Services (MINES for Libraries®): developing an assessment infrastructure for libraries, state, and other types of consortia, presentation to [2nd] Library Assessment Conference, Seattle, http://libraryassessment.org/bm~doc/plum.s.

Rowse, M. (2003) Individual Article Supply: some strategic decisions, *Interlending and document supply*, **31** (2), 86–93.

Singh, R. (2009b) Does your Library have a Marketing Culture? Implications for service providers, *Library Management*, **30** (3), 117–37.

Staines, G. (2009) Towards an Assessment of Strategic Credibility in Academic Libraries, *Library Management*, **30** (3), 148–62.

Suitt, H. (2003) A Blogger in Their Midst, *Harvard Business Review*, **81** (9), September, 30–7.

Chapter 8 Tracking the future

Breeding, M. (2008) An Analytical Approach to Assessing the Effectiveness of Web-based Resources, *Computers in Libraries*, **28** (1), 20–2.

It is very important for libraries and other organizations constantly to strive to create a web presence that is in tune with the needs and expectations of their users. As libraries implement a new design for the website or add in new technology components, it is necessary to accumulate evidence that gauges whether any major change results in a positive or negative impact. There are many different techniques to help a library measure how the technologies it implements live up to user expectations. One approach might be to conduct surveys and focus groups, in which information is gathered from representative samples of the library's users about their interest in a new product or proposed changes. This article discusses techniques that assess the performance of library technologies based on the analysis of use data.

Broady-Preston, J. and Preston, H. (1999) Demonstrating Quality in Academic Libraries, *New Library World*, **100** (1148), 124–9.

Charnigo, L. and Barnett-Ellis, P. (2007) Checking out Facebook.com: the impact of a digital trend on academic libraries, *Information Technology and Libraries*, **26** (1), 23–34.

Dempsey, L. (2009) Always on: libraries in a world of permanent connectivity, *First Monday*, **14** (1–5), January.

Eakin, L. and Pomerantz, J. (2009) Virtual Reference, Real Money: modeling costs in virtual reference services, *Portal: Libraries and the Academy*, **9** (1), (January) 133–64.

Libraries nationwide are in yet another phase of belt tightening. Without an understanding of the economic factors that influence library operations, however, controlling costs and performing cost-benefit analyses on services is difficult. This paper describes a project to develop a cost model for collaborative virtual reference services. This cost model is a systematic description of all expenses incurred by a library in providing virtual reference service as part of a collaborative.

Foster, A. and Ford, N. (2003) Serendipity and Information Seeking: an empirical study, *Journal of Documentation*, **59** (3), 321–40.

Harer, J. B. (2008) Employees as Customers Judging Quality: enhancing employee assessment, *New Library World*, **109** (7/8), 307–20.

The purpose of this paper is to investigate current practices in employee satisfaction assessment to determine if quality in the production of library services and work systems are being assessed from the employees' perspective. It is grounded in the theoretical perspective that customers judge quality and that employees are internal customers, equally important to assessment efforts as are external customers. The paper argues that employees provide a unique perspective to the assessment of quality that external customers cannot provide and that quality assessment needs to be an additional form of employee assessment from that of employee satisfaction or organizational climate initiatives.

Hiller, S., Kyrillidou, M. and Self, J. (2008) When the Evidence is Not Enough: organizational factors that influence effective and successful library assessment, *Performance Measurement and Metrics*, **9** (3), 223–30.

The purpose of this study is to report on the findings of the two-year Association of Research Libraries (ARL) sponsored project, Making Library Assessment Work: Practical Approaches to Effective and Sustainable Assessment; it aims to examine the organizational factors that facilitate and impede effective data use and the implications for assessment in research libraries. Information was gathered from a variety of sources, including: a self-evaluation of assessment activities and needs done by each of the 24 participating libraries; extensive discussion with a designated contact at each library; a review of library and institutional sources such as annual reports, strategic plans, accreditation self-studies, ARL and IPEDS statistics; and the observations and discussion that occurred during 1.5 day site visits. The paper finds that libraries surveyed have made some progress incorporating data in decision making and services improvement, but there is much work to be done. This is not an evidence-based practice study but rather one that examines why evidence (the data on which a decision may be based) is not used more widely in libraries.

Houser, J. C. (2009) The VuFind Implementation at Villanova

University, *Library Hi Tech*, 27 (1).

This case study documents the experiences of Villanova University's Falvey Library staff as they developed and implemented the VuFind open source discovery tool for libraries. It addresses the decision to hire a programmer for the library, the decision to make the VuFind software open source, and the library's development and implementation processes. The author interviewed, recorded and corresponded with seven members of the library staff on multiple occasions over a five-month period, during the ramp-up to, and just after the launch of the new software. This article is complemented by three podcasts created from the interview recordings that are available online. The creators of VuFind took a relatively informal approach to library software development. However, the resulting software was well received, both by the library development community and Villanova University. Keys to this success were close attention to user expectations deriving from experiences using widely available web-based search tools and applications, a continuous process of sharing work and soliciting input, and rapid improvements to the software. The open source development process facilitated the sharing and collaboration that made this rapid improvement possible. Other libraries that are considering the possibility of developing their own software may find Villanova's experience and approach useful in determining where to focus their planning and concentrate their resources. This case study will be of interest to persons engaging in, or considering whether to engage in, open source development of a library application. It will also interest library administrators interested in learning about the technology planning or software development.

Kibbee, J. (2006) Librarians without Borders? Virtual reference service to unaffiliated users, *Journal of Academic Librarianship*, 32 (5), (September), 467–73.

The author investigates issues faced by academic research libraries in providing virtual reference services to unaffiliated users. These libraries generally welcome visitors who use on-site collections and reference services, but are these altruistic policies feasible in a virtual environment? This paper reviews the use of virtual reference service by unaffiliated users to determine their expectations, assess level of demand, and provide recommendations on how libraries should respond. Virtual reference desks can serve their primary constituency and function as a public good for external users if they understand and articulate their role as mediators in the information-seeking process.

Kolsaker, A. and Lee-Kelley, L. (2008) Citizens' Attitudes Towards E-government and E-governance: a UK study, *International Journal of Public Sector Management*, **21** (7), 723–38.
The purpose of this paper is to further understanding of citizens' attitudes towards electronic government (e-government) and e-governance. A quantitative study was conducted of 3000 citizens of a relatively prosperous town in south-east England. A 10% response rate provided 302 completed questionnaires; 216 users of e-government portals and 86 non-users. Findings indicate that although interest in e-government is generally low overall, users appreciate personalization, user-friendliness and the ability to communicate. Users and non-users perceive moderate value in e-government for knowledge acquisition and communication, but little as a vehicle of democratic engagement. Those using e-government frequently are more positive than other groups. The relatively low-response rate (though not unusual for quantitative methods) suggests a general lack of interest; however, users of e-government are appreciative of a few, key benefits. In relation to enhancing participation, the findings suggest that government ambitions far outstrip those of its citizens. To improve usage, the authors propose that non-users need to be tempted online in a secure environment, that users should be provided with personalized pages in line with their expectations, that elected members should be encouraged to view the web as a means of reaching out to voters, and that citizens should be educated in

exploiting the potentially valuable online tools to enhance participation. The study is limited by the exclusive use of quantitative methods; the outcomes suggest that further, qualitative, research could be valuable in exploring user needs, motivations, competence, and level of political engagement.

Latimer, K. and Cranfield, A. (2008) Building for the Future: national and academic libraries from around the globe, report on a conference held in The Hague, 3–5 October 2007, *IFLA Journal*, 34 (4), 359–62.

The International Federation of Library Associations and Institutions' (IFLA) Library Buildings and Equipment Section, in co-operation with Koninklijke Bibliotheek, hosted a conference called Building for the Future in The Hague, Netherlands in October 2007. The aim of the conference was to explore, through a series of visits and case studies, how national and academic library building projects had successfully risen to the challenges posed by raised user expectations and the need for new services. The recent projects from around the world that were discussed and illustrated were innovative and exciting and gave delegates much food for thought.

Martell, C. (2008) The Absent User: physical use of academic libraries and collections continues to decline 1995–2006, *Journal of Academic Librarianship*, 34 (5), (September), 400–7.

Use of the physical collections and services of academic libraries continues to plummet, with some exceptions, while use of electronic networked resources skyrockets. This article frames the extent of this decline with a focus on circulation and reference among ARL university, medical and law libraries, the Ivy League, other associations, systems and individual libraries.

Moore, A. C. and Wells, K. A. (2009) Connecting 24/5 to Millennials: providing academic support services from a learning commons, *Journal of Academic Librarianship*, 35 (1), 75–85.

Ojala, M. (2006) Rethinking Collections, Libraries, and Information, *Online*, 30 (1), 5.

Owen, T. (2006) *Success at the Enquiry Desk*, 5th edn, Facet

Publishing, ISBN 978-1-85604-600-8.

Pantry, S. and Griffiths, P. (2001) *The Complete Guide to Preparing and Implementing Service Level Agreements*, 2nd edn, Library Association Publishing, ISBN 978-1-85604-410-6.

Pesenti, J. (2008) The Search Gap, *Information Today*, 25 (5), 20.
Most internet-savvy people prefer a web search engine over a search engine behind a firewall (that is, to find information only available inside one's organization). Outside the firewall, search has allowed efficient collaboration and the exchange of valuable information between people with absolutely no prior connection. This allows anybody to mine and leverage collective wisdom and creates an incentive to augment it. Inside the firewall, where interests are much closer and exchanges could be even more valuable, such interactions through search have not happened. People need search, yet they do not use it at all. To search behind a firewall effectively, one needs a search engine that is good enough to start a virtuous circle. This means resolving issues related to coverage, findability and usability, which should lead to higher usage, raised user expectations, higher information technology focus, and better searching.

Rooney-Browne, C. (2008) Changing the Way We Look at Libraries?: an evaluation of East Renfrewshire's Look at Libraries festival, *Library Review*, 57 (1), 50–66.
The current financial and political climate means that libraries are more accountable to their stakeholders and are under increasing pressure to justify their place and value in an ever-changing information society. The purpose of this report is to discuss how one local library and information service has adapted to changes in cultural demands and user expectations to deliver a concept that communicates its social value to all of its stakeholders. The report combines quantitative and qualitative research techniques to determine the outputs and outcomes of the project and to assess if key objectives have been achieved. The results of this evaluation confirm that the Look at Libraries festival has been embraced by event attendees, staff, participants

and the community. The research also illustrates that the demands and expectations of two communities can vary dramatically, posing the question: is it right to judge libraries so heavily on their outputs? The emerging impact of the festival also supports the argument that the local library service can support its parent body to achieve overall community objectives. The research was conducted during a four-week academic placement period within East Renfrewshire Council Library and Information Service. The depth of the research has been challenged by limitations associated with time and resources. Therefore, the findings must be viewed as preliminary and suggestive rather than exhaustive. The case study reveals an innovative approach by a public library and information service to challenge perceptions, communicate changes in service provision, market public libraries, attract new members and establish an effective brand extension for the service.

Ryan, S. M. (2008) Reference Transactions Analysis: the cost-effectiveness of staffing a traditional academic reference desk, *Journal of Academic Librarianship*, **34** (5), 389–99.

This study categorizes 6959 reference desk transactions to determine how many of the queries require the attention of a librarian. Results indicate that 89% could likely be answered by non-librarians. From the results of this and other studies, the author explores the cost-effectiveness of staffing a traditional reference desk with librarians.

Vondracek, R. (2007) Comfort and Convenience? Why students choose alternatives to the Library, *Portal: Libraries and the Academy*, **7** (3), 277–93.

Oregon State University (OSU) researchers surveyed 3227 undergraduate students to identify how many students use or do not use the physical and virtual OSU libraries. Most importantly, they wanted to determine the alternatives to the library that students choose for typical library activities, such as studying, research, and research assistance, and why they prefer those alternatives. A total of 275 (29%) of the 949 respondents identified themselves as infrequent or non-users of the physical and/or virtual library. The researchers conducted focus groups with both library users and non-users, and surveyed 95 (35%) of the infrequent and non-users. The results suggest that students seek comfort, convenience and quiet in extra-library and library environments; rely on knowledgeable individuals for research assistance; and conduct the majority of their research online from home.

Wang, J. and Lim, A. (2009) Local Touch and Global Reach: the next generation of network-level information discovery and delivery services in a digital landscape, *Library Management*, 30 (1–2), 25–34.

Technology changes swiftly and the traditional library online public access catalogue (OPAC) is in danger of becoming irrelevant as more users rely on network-level search engines such as Google and Google Scholar to search for information resources. This paper seeks to explore the next-generation discovery and delivery solutions that are designed to adapt to changing user expectations in the Web 2.0 environment. It aims to examine the current trends in which libraries are partnering with vendors to promote their value-added services to library users, and are making their collections more visible in a global digital landscape. The paper begins with an overview of current library catalogues and then introduces some emerging products focusing on discovery and delivery that affect the value of libraries as they present their collections and provide services to a new generation of library users. Case studies are presented to illustrate trendy features of next-generation catalogues as well as the challenges that the new tools bring to libraries as they work toward providing users with richer discovery experiences and greater delivery of content beyond local collections. The paper identifies major problems with libraries' existing OPACs as well as challenges of implanting new discovery tools to meet the demands of today's network users. It suggests that libraries must become more responsive and adaptable to remain sustainable, relevant and competitive in the new environment. The paper presents an up-to-date account of the state of next-generation library catalogues used in American libraries.

White, L. N. (2008) Aligning Library Assessment Processes to the Library's Service Environment: a conceptual model, *Library Review*, 57 (7), 499–513.

Libraries can improve the reporting and value of their assessment processes by improving the alignment of their assessment processes in two ways: internally through the use of consistent and innovative processes, metrics and culture within the library, and externally by embracing the alignment factors of the library's service environment. The library must develop more effective assessment alignment processes by progressively elevating the alignment of the library's assessment processes from internal non-alignment of assessment to the total alignment of assessment to the library' service environment and the dynamic environmental factors driving today's libraries.

Chapter 9 Future perfect?

Albanese, A. R. (2006) The Heart of Texas: with the University of Texas Libraries, wherever you go, there they are, *Library Journal*, 131 (19), 36.

In 2005 the University of Texas (UT) at Austin made some surprising national headlines when it removed the book collection from its undergraduate library. Behind the sensational headlines, the move was in fact more life-as-usual than radical change. In today's academic libraries, technology is constantly redefining library services and space, and UT has been one of the nation's most innovative libraries in seizing the digital moment. While national headlines made the removal of a book collection from what is now the Flawn Academic Center (FAC) seem like a milestone in library history, renovating the FAC was welcomed heartily by the UT students. This article describes how the new FAC allows users to access the library services wherever they are.

This article also describes the impact of the FAC renovation on students.

Ayris, P. (2008) The Library as Place – What Users Want, presentation at Partnership in Academic Excellence, UNICA Scholarly Communications Seminar, Prague, www.ulb.ac.be/unica/docs/Sch-com-2008-Paul_Ayris_2.t.

Bainton, T. (2009) A Zest for Reinvention: themes of the Society of College, National and Universities' conference, 10–12 June, Bournemouth UK. *Library+Information Gazette*, 22 May–4 June, 5.

Brophy, P. et al. (eds) (2004) *Libraries Without Walls 5: the delivery of library services to distance users*, Facet Publishing, ISBN 978-1-85604-511-7.

Brophy, P. et al. (eds) (2006) *Libraries Without Walls 6: evaluating the distributed delivery of library services*, Facet Publishing, ISBN 978-1-85604-576-6.

Brophy, P. et al. (eds) (2008) *Libraries Without Walls 7: exploring 'anytime', 'anywhere' delivery of library services*, Facet Publishing, ISBN 978-1-85604-623-7.

Carlson, S. (2001) The Deserted Library: as students work online, reading rooms empty out – leading some campuses to add Starbucks, *Chronicle of Higher Education*, **48** (12), A35–8.

Chowdhury, G. G. and Chowdhury, S. (2010) *Information Users and Usability in the Digital Age*, Facet Publishing, ISBN 978-1-85604-597-1 (in press).

CIBER (2008) Information behaviour of the researcher of the future [executive summary], University College London, www.ucl.ac.uk/infostudies/research/ciber/downloads/ ggexecutive.pdf.

Coffman, S. (1998) What if You Ran Your Library Like a Bookstore? *American Libraries*, **29** (3), 40–6.

Cooke, R. (2007) Fiction Belongs in Libraries – Not in Council Policy, *Observer*, 26 August, www.guardian.co.uk/books/2007/aug/26/features.review.

Cooper, L. (2005) *Modern Library Management: the changing role*

of the ILS, [n.p], Talis,
www.talis.com/applications/downloads/white_papers/
TheChangingRoleoftheILS.pdf.

Council on Library and Information Resources (2005) *Library as Place: rethinking roles, rethinking space*, ISBN 1-932326-13-8. The text of the report is available free on CLIR's website at www.clir.org/pubs/abstract/pub129abst.html. Print copies can be ordered for $20 per copy plus shipping at www.clir.org/pubs/execsum/sum129.html.

DCMS (2000) *Comprehensive, Efficient and Modern Public Libraries: standards and assessment*, DCMS, www.culture.gov.uk/PDF/libraries_pls_assess.pdf.

Deegan, M. and Tanner, S. (2001) *Digital Futures*, Facet Publishing, ISBN 978-1-85604-580-3.

Deegan, M. and Tanner, S. (2006) *Digital Preservation*, Facet Publishing, ISBN 978-1-85604-485-1.

Foster, A. (2008) Battening Down the Hatches: business information survey 2009, *Business Information Review*, **26** (1) 10–27.

Frey, T. (2006) *The Future of Libraries: future scenario, historical perspective, technology trends*, 2 November, www.futuristspeaker.com/2006/11/the-future-of-libraries.

Griffiths, J. R. and Craven, J. (eds) (2008) *Access, Delivery, Performance: the future of libraries without walls*, Facet Publishing, ISBN 978-1-85604-647-3.

Hallworth, F. (1972) Public Libraries and Resource Centres, *Library Association Record*, **74** (3), March, 39–41.

Hughes, L. M. (2004) *Digitizing Collections*, Facet Publishing, ISBN 978-1-85604-466-0.

Johnson, H. (1994) Strategic Planning for Modern Libraries, *Library Management*, **15** (1), 7–18.

Joint, N. (2009b) Choosing Between Print or Digital Collection Building in Times of Financial Constraint, *New Library World*, **58** (4), 264–71.

Kova, M. (2008) *Never Mind the Web: here comes the book*, Oxford, Chandos.

McMenemy, D. and Poulter, A. (2005) *Delivering Digital Services*, Facet Publishing, ISBN 978-1-85604-510-0.

Midgley, S. (2009) Shush, This Is a Digital Library, *Times* (Postgraduates supplement), 23 April, 5, http://business.timesonline.co.uk/tol/business/career_and_jobs/article6154172.ece.

MLA (2009) *Shaping a Modern Library Service* [by Roy Clare], www.mla.gov.uk/en/news_and_views/views/wirral_comment.aspx.

Needham, G. and Ally, M. (2008) *M-Libraries: libraries on the move to provide virtual access*, Facet Publishing, ISBN 978-1-85604-648-0.

Nicholas, D. and Rowlands, I. (eds) (2008) *Digital Consumers: reshaping the information professions*, Facet Publishing, ISBN 978-1-85604-651-0.

Ojala, M. (2006) Rethinking Collections, Libraries, and Information, *Online*, **30** (1), 5, www.infotoday.com/online/jan06/HomePage.shtml.

Pantry, S. and Griffiths, P. (2003) *Your Essential Guide to Career Success*, Facet Publishing, ISBN 978-1-85604-491-2.

Pantry, S. and Griffiths, P. (2004) *Managing Outsourcing in Library and Information Services*, Facet Publishing, ISBN 978-1-85604-543-8.

Pomerantz, J. and Marchionini, G. (2007) The Digital Library as Place, *Journal of Documentation*, **63** (4), 505–33.

Rowlands, I. and Nicholas, D. (2008) Understanding Information Behaviour: how do students and faculty find books? *Journal of Academic Librarianship*, **34** (1), 3–15.

Ross, L. and Sennvey, P. (2008) The Library Is Dead, Long Live the Library!: the practice of academic librarianship and the digital revolution, *Journal of Academic Librarianship*, **34** (2), 145–52. As a direct consequence of the digital revolution, academic libraries today face competition as information providers. Using Richard N. Foster's technology S curves as the analytical model, this article shows that academic libraries are in the midst of discontinuous change by questioning a number of assumptions that support the current practice of academic librarianship. The authors challenge these assumptions, and analyse the manner in which digital communications affect academic libraries.

Self, W. (2007) Give Me Books in my Library, not Coffee, the Net and DVDs. *Evening Standard* [London], 23 October, www.thisislondon.co.uk/standard/article-23417818-details/Give+me+books+in+my+library,+not+coffee,+the+net+and+DVDs/article.do.

Sinikara, K. (2008) *Users Evaluating Library Space and Services: case study from the University of Helsinki*, presentation at Partnership in Academic Excellence, UNICA Scholarly Communications Seminar, Prague, www.ulb.ac.be/unica/docs/Sch-com-2008-Kaisa_Sinikara.t.

Tenopir, C., King, D. W., Edwards, S. and Wu, L. (2009) Electronic Journals and Changes in Scholarly Article Seeking and Reading Patterns, *Aslib Proceedings: New Information Perspectives*, **61** (1), 5–32.

By tracking the information-seeking and reading patterns of science, technology, medical and social science faculty members from 1977 to the present, this paper seeks to examine how faculty members locate, obtain, read and use scholarly articles and how this has changed with the widespread availability of electronic journals and journal alternatives. Data were gathered using questionnaire surveys of university faculty and other researchers periodically since 1977. Many questions used the critical incident of the last article reading to allow analysis of the characteristics of readings in addition to characteristics of readers. The paper finds that the average number of readings per year per science faculty member continues to increase, while the average time spent per reading is decreasing. Electronic articles now account for the majority of readings, though most readings are still printed on paper for final reading. Scientists report reading a higher proportion of older articles from a wider range of journal titles and more articles from library e-collections. Articles are read for many purposes and readings are valuable to those purposes. The paper draws on data collected in a consistent way over 30 years. It provides a unique look at how electronic journals and other developments have influenced changes in reading behaviour over three decades. The use of critical incidence provides evidence of the value of reading in addition to reading patterns.

Todd, J. L. (2008) GIS and Libraries: a cross-disciplinary approach, *Online*, **32** (5), 14–18.

Venkatraman, A. (2009) Educators Look to Uncover Research Habits of the Crossover Generation, *Information World Review*, 253 (March), 6, available online with the title *Educators Study Research Habits of Generation Y* at www.iwr.co.uk/information-world-review/analysis/2238090/educators-uncover-research.

Virkus, S. et al. (2009) Integration of digital libraries and virtual learning environments: a literature review, *New Library World*, **110** (3/4), 136–50.

Waxman, L. et al. (2007) The Library as Place: providing students with opportunities for socialization, relaxation and restoration, *New Library World*, **108** (9/10), 424–34.

Westwood, R. (2009) Playing to our Strengths, *Library + Information Gazette*, 8 May–21 May 2009, 5, www.robwestwood.co.uk/2009/06/04/a-retail-model-we-can-depend-on.

Wilson, M. (2000) Understanding the Needs of Tomorrow's Library User: rethinking library services for the new age, *Australian Public Libraries and Information Services*, **13** (2), 81–6, http://search.informit.com.au/documentSummary;dn=98343468 2974176;res=IELHSS.

Woodward, J. (2009) *Creating the Customer-Driven Academic Library*, American Library Association, ISBN 978-0-8389-0976-8. Academic libraries are going through what may be the most difficult period in their history. With more and more scholarly content available online and accessible almost anywhere, where does the traditional brick and mortar library fit in? In this book Jeannette Woodward attacks these and other pressing issues facing today's academic librarians. Her trailblazing strategies centre on keeping the customer's point of view in focus at all times to help you:

- integrate technology to meet today's student and faculty needs
- revaluate the role and function of library service desks
- implement staffing strategies to match customer expectations
- create new and effective promotional materials.

Librarians are now faced with marketing to a generation of students who log on rather than walk in and this cutting-edge book supplies the tools needed to keep customers coming through the door.

Web resource

www.librarysupportstaff.com/strategicplan.html.

Appendix 2
Where to go for further information

Professional bodies

The following list includes brief descriptions, contact details and other information about a range of national and international professional bodies that can help to provide you with relevant news and research that will keep your knowledge and skills up to date. A number of them provide access to their professional resources and publishing, either selectively or by providing free access after a period of time (typically 2–3 years after publication). Members may have additional access, for example, CILIP members are provided with electronic access to a range of professional journals through Emerald, and to two refereed journals, which are hosted by Sage.

UK

Aslib, The Association for Information Management
207 Davina House
137–49 Goswell Road
London EC1V 7ET
Tel: +44 (0) 20 7253 3349
Fax: +44 (0) 20 7490 0577
E-mail: aslib@aslib.com
www.aslib.co.uk
Offers corporate, affiliate and student membership and group and branches that form an international network of information professionals

in every sector of the information world.

Publications include: *Journal of Documentation, Aslib Proceedings, Program* (available through the Emerald aggregation platform www.emeraldinsight.com), *Managing Information* (www. managinginformation.com).

Offers *Aslib Management Knowledge Resource,* a tailored version of Emerald *ManagementFirst* website designed to meet the needs of Aslib's corporate members.

British Library (BL)
St Pancras
96 Euston Road
London NW1 2DB
Tel: +44 (0) 870 444 1500
E-mail: Customer-Services@bl.uk
www.bl.uk

The British Library (BL)
Boston Spa
Wetherby
West Yorkshire LS23 7BQ

British Library Newspapers
Colindale Avenue
London NW9 5HE
There is an extensive list of specific contact details at www.bl.uk/aboutus/contact/index.html.

Chartered Institute of Marketing (CIM)
Moor Hall
Cookham
Maidenhead
Berkshire SL6 9QH
Tel: +44 (0) 1628 427500
Fax: +44 (0) 1628 427499

E-mail: see http://omega.cim.co.uk/ContactUs.aspx
www.cim.co.uk
'As the world's largest organisation for professional marketers the CIM play a key role in training, developing and representing their profession.'
 Publication: *The Marketer*

Chartered Institute of Personnel and Development (CIPD)
151 The Broadway
London SW19 1JQ
Tel: +44 (0) 20 8612 6200
Fax: +44 (0) 20 8612 6201
E-mail: see www.cipd.co.uk/contactus/
www.cipd.co.uk
'The CIPD is the professional body for those involved in the management and development of people.'
 Publication: *People Management* (www.peoplemanagement. co.uk/pm/)

Chartered Management Institute (CMI)
Management House
Cottingham Road
Corby
Northamptonshire NN17 1TT
Tel: +44 (0)1536 204 222
Fax: +44 (0)1536 201 651
www.managers.org.uk
'The Chartered Management Institute is the only chartered professional body that is dedicated to management and leadership. We are committed to raising the performance of business by championing management. We do this through supporting and advising individuals and organisations, or through engaging policy makers and key influencers in government and the management profession.'
 Publication: *Professional Manager*. Also publishes a range of 220 management checklists.

CILIP: the Chartered Institute of Library and Information Professionals

7 Ridgmount Street
London WC1E 7AE
Tel: +44 (0) 20 7255 0500
Fax: +44(0) 20 7255 0581
E-mail: info@cilip.org.uk
www.cilip.org.uk
Professional body for information and library staff; offers advice, guidance and training.

Publications: *Library and Information Update, Library and Information Gazette*; access to *Journal of Information Science* (JIS), *Journal of Librarianship and Information Science* (JOLIS) and *Library and Information Science Abstracts* (LISA).

Links on the website to CILIP special interest groups, regional branches, and representatives in the UK devolved nations (CILIP Cymru/Wales, CILIPS (CILIP Scotland) and CILIP in Ireland), and to many of their journals.

Facet Publishing

7 Ridgmount Street
London WC1E 7AE
Tel: +44 (0) 20 7255 0500
Fax: +44(0) 20 7255 0581
E-mail: info@facetpublishing.co.uk
www.facetpublishing.co.uk
'Publishing arm of CILIP: the Chartered Institute of Library and Information Professionals, Facet Publishing is the home to the world's leading resources for information professionals worldwide.'

Museums, Libraries and Archives Council (MLA)

Head office is based in Birmingham and there is also an office in London.

Birmingham:
The Museums, Libraries and Archives Council
Grosvenor House
14 Bennetts Hill
Birmingham B2 5RS
Tel: +44 (0)121 345 7300
Fax: +44 (0)121 345 7303
E-mail: info@mla.gov.uk or via www.mla.gov.uk/en/about/who/
    staff.aspx
www.mla.gov.uk

London:
The Museums, Libraries and Archives Council
Wellcome Wolfson Building
165 Queen's Gate
South Kensington
London SW7 5HD
Tel: +44 (0)20 7273 1444
Fax: +44 (0)20 7273 1404
www.mla.org.uk
'Leading strategically, the MLA promotes best practice in museums,
libraries and archives, to inspire innovative, integrated and
sustainable services for all.

A non-departmental public body (NDPB), sponsored by the UK
Department for Culture, Media and Sport (DCMS). Launched in
April 2000 as the strategic body working with and for the
museums, archives and libraries sector, tapping into the potential
for collaboration between them, MLA replaced the Museums and
Galleries Commission (MGC) and the Library and Information
Commission (LIC).'

Publications: listed at www.mla.gov.uk/what/publications

Publishers Association (PA)

29b Montague Street
London WC1B 5BW

Tel: +44 (0)20 7691 9191
Fax: +44 (0)20 7691 9199
E-mail: mail@publishers.org.uk
www.publishers.org.uk
'The PA's mission is to strengthen the trading environment for UK
publishers, by providing a strong voice for the industry in
government, within society and with other stakeholders in the UK,
in Europe and internationally; providing a forum for the exchange
of non-competitive information between publishers; and providing
support and guidance to the industry through technological and
other changes. PA's core service is representation and lobbying,
around copyright, rights and other matters relevant to our
members, who represent roughly 80 per cent of the industry by
turnover.'

Ireland

The Library Association of Ireland (LAI) (Cumann Leabharlann na hÉireann)

53 Upper Mount Street
Dublin 2
Ireland
www.libraryassociation.ie
Publication: *An Leabharlann*: *The Irish Library*
(www.anleabharlann.ie/) 'Journal of the LAI and CILIP Ireland'

Australasia

Australian Library and Information Association (ALIA)

Postal Address: PO Box 6335 Kingston 2604 Australia
ALIA House, 9–11 Napier Close, Deakin 2600 Australia
Tel: +61 2 6215 8222
Fax: +61 2 6282 2249
E-mail: enquiry@alia.org.au
www.alia.org.au

The Australian Library and Information Association (ALIA) is the professional organization for the Australian library and information services sector. It seeks to empower the profession in the development, promotion and delivery of quality library and information services to the nation, through leadership, advocacy and mutual support.

Publications: *Australian Library Journal* (ARJ; www.alia.org.au/publishing/alj/), *Australian Academic and Research Libraries* (AARL; www.alia.org.au/publishing/aarl/)

Australian Publishers Association (APA)

60/89 Jones Street, Ultimo, New South Wales 2007
Tel: +61 2 9281 9788
Fax: +61 2 9281 1073
E-mail: apa@publishers.asn.au
www.publishers.asn.au

'The Australian Publishers Association (APA) is the peak industry body for Australian book, journal and electronic publishers. Established in 1948, the association is an advocate for all Australian publishers: large or small; commercial or non-profit; academic or popular; locally or overseas owned.

Over the years the APA has grown into an organisation of considerable influence. From modest beginnings and a membership of twenty, the Association now has over 160 members and represents 91% of the industry, based on turnover.'

Book Publishers Association of New Zealand (BPANZ)

Postal address: P O Box 102 006, North Shore 0745, Auckland, New Zealand
4 Whetu Place. Mairangi Bay, North Shore City, Auckland 0632, New Zealand
Tel: +64-9-477-5589
Fax: +64-9-477-5570
E-mail: admin@bpanz.org.nz
www.bpanz.org.nz

'The Book Publishers Association of New Zealand is the organisation that represents the publishing industry and acts as an advocate for all publishers. In addition to our book publisher members we offer associate memberships to designers, distributors, literary agents and printers.

BPANZ has been serving the New Zealand book publishing industry for thirty years and has played a key role in many of the changes and improvements we've seen over that time. As well as representing the industry, we offer opportunities for people in this field to meet with colleagues in both formal and informal situations. BPANZ has approximately 100 members consisting of book publishers, distributors, printers and designers.'

There are proposals to change the name of BPANZ by dropping the word 'book' or by changing it to 'Publishers New Zealand'.

Publication: *The Publisher* (http://bpanz.org.nz/?page_id=12)

New Zealand Library Association (LIANZA)

Postal address: PO Box 12–212, Thorndon, Wellington 6144, New Zealand

Level 7, Navigate House, 69 Boulcott Street, Wellington 6011, New Zealand

Tel: +64 4 473 5834

Fax: +64 4 499 1480

E-mail: admin@lianza.org.nz

www.lianza.org.nz

Publications: *New Zealand Library and Information Management Journal, Library Life*

North America

American Library Association (ALA)

ALA provides leadership for the development, promotion and improvement of library and information services and the profession of librarianship in order to enhance learning and ensure access to information for all.

The ALA has its headquarters in Chicago IL but also many offices around the USA; see www.ala.org for full details.

Publication: *American Libraries* (monthly) (www.ala.org/ala/alonline/index.cfm)

Association of American Publishers (AAP)

Association of American Publishers, Inc.
50 F Street, NW
4th Floor
Washington, DC 20001
Tel: +1 202.347.3375
Fax: +1 202.347.3690
E-mail: jplatt@publishers.org, aoconnor@publishers.org
www.publishers.org
'The Association of American Publishers (AAP), representing publishers of all sizes and types located throughout the country, is the principal trade association of the U.S. book publishing industry'.

Publication: *Professional/Scholarly Publishing Bulletin*

Canadian Library Association (CLA)/Association canadienne des bibliothèques (ACB)

328 Frank Street
Ottawa, ON K2P 0X8
Canada
Tel: +1(613) 232-9625
Fax: +1(613) 563-9895
E-mail: info@cla.ca
www.cla.ca
'CLA/ACB is my advocate and public voice, educator and network. We build the Canadian library and information community and advance its information professionals.'

Publications: *Feliciter, CLA Digest*

Canadian Publishers Council (CPC)

250 Merton Street
Suite 203
Toronto M4S 1B1
Canada
Tel: +1 (416) 322 7011
Fax: +1 (416) 322 6999
E-mail: pubadmin@pubcouncil.ca
www.pubcouncil.ca

'The Canadian Publishers' Council, as Canada's main English language book publishing trade association was founded in 1910 and represents the interests of publishing companies that publish books and other media for elementary and secondary schools, colleges and universities, professional and reference markets, the retail and library sectors. Members employ more than 2800 Canadians and collectively account for nearly three-quarters of all domestic sales of English-language books.

The Council represents the Canadian publishing community on the international level in the International Publishers Association (IPA) and is a member of the International Federation of Reprographic Rights Organizations (IFFRO). The CPC also maintains liaison with other Canadian professional publishers' associations, with the Association of American Publishers and the U.K. Publishers Association, as well as with Canadian colleagues in all areas of the literary arts, educational, library and retail communities.'

South Africa

Library and Information Association of South Africa (LIASA)

LIASA National Office
Vista Campus
263 Skinner Street
Pretoria Central
PO Box 1598

Pretoria 0001
South Africa
Tel: +27 (0) 12 337 6129
Fax: +27 (0) 12 337 6108
E-mail: liasa@liasa.org.za
www.liasa.org.za
Publication: *South African Journal of Libraries and Information Science*

Publishers' Association of South Africa (PASA)

Unit 305, 2nd floor, The Foundry
Prestwich Street
Green Point 8005
South Africa
Postal address @ PO Box 106, Green Point 8051
Tel: +27 (0) 21 425 2721
Fax: +27 (0) 21 421 3270
E-mail: pasa@publishsa.co.za
www.publishsa.co.za
'PASA is the largest publishing industry association in South Africa, committed to creativity, literacy, the free flow of ideas and encourages a culture of reading.'
　　Publications: *Position Papers* are available online at www.publishsa.co.za/home.php?cmd=about_pa_popaper.

International

EBLIDA: European Bureau of Library Information and Documentation Associations

Grote Marktstraat 43
2511 BH The Hague
The Netherlands
Tel: +31 70 309 0551
Fax: +31 70 309 0558
E-mail: eblida@debibliotheken.nl

www.eblida.org
At the time of going to press (May 2009) the EBLIDA Secretariat is provided by the Dutch Public Library Association (Vereniging Openbare Bibliotheken) whose postal address is Postbus 16146, 2500 BC Den Haag [The Hague], Netherlands.

'EBLIDA is the European Bureau of Library, Information and Documentation Associations. We are an independent umbrella association of national library, information, documentation and archive associations and institutions in Europe.

Subjects on which EBLIDA concentrates are European information society issues, including copyright & licensing, culture & education and EU enlargement. We promote unhindered access to information in the digital age and the role of archives and libraries in achieving this goal.'

EBLIDA's members are national associations for librarianship, information science and archives management; commercial organizations can also be sponsors but have no voting rights. Its publications provide an overview of activity by European information associations on major information society initiatives.

Publications: *Eblida News* (www.eblida.org/index.php?page= eblida-update). Until December 2006 this was known as *Eblida Hot News*.

The International Federation of Library Associations and Institutions (IFLA)

PO Box 95312
2509 CH The Hague
Netherlands
Tel: +31 70 3140884
Fax: +31 70 3834827
E-mail: ifla@ifla.org
www.ifla.org
'The International Federation of Library Associations and Institutions (IFLA) is the leading international body representing the interests of library and information services and their users. It is

the global voice of the library and information profession.'

Publications: *IFLA Journal* (available through www.ifla.org/en/ifla-publications).

Special Libraries Association (SLA)

331 South Patrick Street
Alexandria
VA 22314-3501
USA
Tel: +1.703.647.4900
Fax: +1.703.647.4901
E-mail: various contacts are listed at
www.sla.org/content/SLA/contactus/index.cfm#execoffice
www.sla.org
'Through innovative learning, successful networking, and effective advocacy, SLA is a connective force for the profession.'

Publication: *Information Outlook*

Subscription agents

Association of Subscription Agents and Intermediaries (ASAI)

Sarah Durrant
Secretary General
Field Cottage
School Lane
Benhall
Suffolk IP17 1HE
Tel: +44 (0)1728 633196
E-mail: sarah@redsage.org
www.subscription-agents.org/
Subscription agents and intermediaries help libraries and publishers save money. They reduce the amount of time spent on the many detailed administrative tasks in acquiring and accessing journals, thus allowing librarians and publishers to focus their attention on other

important matters. In the process they perform these administrative tasks more cheaply than would otherwise be the case.

Intermediaries help publishers and libraries alike reduce the costs of producing, distributing, managing and accessing their electronic journal and information services.

Check the Association of Subscription Agents website (www.subscription-agents.org/members.html) for a listing of many subscription agents but here are some of the major ones:

Ebsco
www.ebsco.com

Otto Harrassowitz
www.harrassowitz.de

Ingenta
www.ingenta.com

Karger Libri
www.libri.ch

Maruzen
www.maruzen.co.jp

Prenax
www.prenax.com

Swets
www.swets.com

Wolper
www.wolper.com

Index